Fantastic
Garlands

Fantastic Garlands

An Anthology of
Flowers and Plants
from Shakespeare

Lys de Bray

Lys de Bray

BLANDFORD PRESS
POOLE   DORSET

First published in U.K. 1982 by Blandford Press, Link House, West Street, Poole, Dorset, BH15 1LL

Copyright © 1982 Blandford Books Ltd.

Distributed in the United States by Sterling Publishing Co., Inc., 2 Park Avenue, New York, N.Y. 10016

British Library Cataloguing in Publication Data
de Bray, Lys
   Fantastic garlands.
     1. Shakespeare, William –
Knowledge – Botany
     2. Flowers in literature
     I. Title
     822.3'3   PR3041

ISBN 0 7137 1066 7

Typeset in 11/12 point Monophoto Garamond by Keyspools Ltd, Bridge Street, Golborne, Lancs.

Printed in Singapore by Toppan Printing Co. (S) Pte.

Contents

Foreword by Dr Levi Fox, Director of the
Shakespeare Birthplace Trust   vii

Preface   ix

Acknowledgements   x

Introduction   xi

The Plates   14–141

Index of Shakespeare's Plant Names   142

Index of Latin Names   143

Bibliography   144

There with fantastic garlands did she come
Of crow-flowers, nettles, daisies, and long purples,
That liberal shepherds give a grosser name,
But our cold maids do dead men's fingers call them:

Foreword

By Dr Levi Fox, OBE

Director of the Shakespeare Birthplace Trust

For one who has been concerned with Shakespeare and flowers for many years it is a particular pleasure to introduce and commend this handsome book.

One of the many varied responsibilities which I have enjoyed as Director of the Shakespeare Birthplace Trust has been the supervision of the gardens of the Shakespearian properties, where trees, flowers and herbs mentioned in Shakespeare's plays attract the attention and admiration of visitors from all over the world. I have been fortunate in that I have thus had an unusual opportunity to indulge an instinctive love of flowers which I owe to my upbringing in the country. Indeed the rural environment of my boyhood was in many respects very like the Warwickshire countryside of Shakespeare's time.

I have also had much to do with gardeners and have come to appreciate the sterling qualities and skill of those who devote their lives to carrying on the centuries-old tradition of the gardener's craft. In particular I recall with affection a former head gardener who had served the Birthplace Trust for over fifty years. He was a man such as Shakespeare himself might well have employed in his own garden at New Place. His sense of duty and loyalty savoured of an age that has passed. He had an encyclopaedic knowledge, based on experience and not books, of all the trees, plants, flowers and herbs which would have been found in the gardens of Elizabethan England and which he tended with an almost reverential devotion in the gardens of Shakespeare's Birthplace, Anne Hathaway's Cottage and New Place. He could practise the processes of pruning and grafting so accurately described by Shakespeare and like the poet himself knew everything about the properties of herbs and the hazards of weeds, blights and frosts. He was a Warwickshire man, born and bred, and what impressed me especially was his use of words and phrases when describing flowers and garden matters that might well have been current in Shakespeare's time. Indeed after talking to him one could have no doubt that only a Warwickshire man familiar with knott gardens, orchards, riverside meadows and country scenes could possibly have written Shakespeare's plays.

Of Shakespeare's own love and knowledge of flowers, plants and herbs and of his delight in the natural scenery of his native Warwickshire there is ample evidence in his plays and sonnets. As with his profound understanding of human character, so with his knowledge of the processes of nature; the poet's acute power of observation and sympathy were matched with the genius not only to describe what he saw in unforgettable poetic language, but to convey in happy phrase and touching epithet something of the inner meaning and mystery of their loveliness.

It is not surprising that Shakespeare's flowers continue to be a subject of absorbing interest, not just for horticulturalists and botanists but for all who have an instinctive appreciation of natural beauty. In the pages that follow Lys de Bray illuminates this subject in an appealing manner, presenting an unusual combination of informed commentary and artistic skill, and at the same time using to full advantage Shakespeare's own exquisite descriptions. Of similar books I know none which has made me more aware of the symbolism of individual flowers and plants and of Shakespeare's rich legacy of floral imagery.

The Shakespeare Centre,
Stratford-upon-Avon

Preface

SHAKESPEARE named about 180 different flowers, trees, fruit and vegetables in his writings; I have arranged these in groups (or as occasional single paintings) and, as far as possible, in seasonal order. The quotations gave me much pleasure in the choosing – and some difficulty too, because where several extracts appear on one page it was necessary to select those plants that associated well with each other in their natural habitat, that flowered at approximately the same time, and with a similar scenario in the play or sonnet.

All the plants were painted in their appropriate seasons, with the exception of the tropical subjects, and several of the flowers have never been included in an anthology of this kind before.

Because of the uncertainty of being able to find all the plants and flowers at the right time, it was a necessary pleasure to grow as many of these as possible in order to have them to hand for their sometimes all-too-brief flowering time. For two years, my garden was a strange and curious confusion of wild flowers, seeds, bulbs, vegetables, roses and border plants, and among the every-day cottage garden flowers such as Pansies and Marigolds or 'Mary-buds' I grew the following, which are listed under the names by which Shakespeare would have known them: Corn Cockle, Oxlip, Holy Thistle, Crown Imperial, Columbine, Eglantine, Coloquintida, Pinks, Lilies, Carnations, 'Insane Root', 'Aconitum', Leek, Angelica, Violet, Wild Daffodil, Narcissus, Nettle, Lords-and-Ladies or Cuckoo-Pint, Pignut, 'Cuckoo-bud', Dewberry, Briar, Rue, Sedge, Rush, 'Furrow Weeds', Docks, Thistles, 'Kecksies', Burs, Flax, Wormwood, Poppy (Opium), Balm, Plantain, 'Honey Stalks', 'Love-in-Idleness', Mallow, Knot Grass, Pimpernel, Blackberry, Bean, Lettuce, Hyssop, Lavender, Radish, Caraway, Wild Strawberry and Saffron.

Extra roses such as that old favourite 'Rosa Mundi', and R. centifolia 'Tour de Malakoff', R. damascena 'Ispahan' and the moss centifolia 'William Lobb' came to stay. By their lasting presence they will always remind me of those two very busy years when I painted many hundreds of flowers separately before amalgamating them to make up the following plates portraying Shakespeare's flowers.

The quotations throughout the book have been taken from The Temple Shakespeare, Cambridge edition, printed by J. M. Dent in 1895. Exact references may differ in other editions. The Two Noble Kinsmen was written by Shakespeare in collaboration with John Fletcher. Editions available are the New Penguin Shakespeare edition (Penguin 1977) and the Regents Renaissance Drama Series edition (ed. G. R. Proudfoot, Edward Arnold 1970).

My own text is an assortment of horticultural information, plant-history, myths, legends and herbal knowledge, which has had to be tailored to fit the length of the quotations chosen.

Lys de Bray (1981)

Acknowledgements

MY most sincere and grateful thanks are due to the following kind people, without whose help this book could not have been illustrated so fully and completely. Many were able to give me the rarer plant-specimens from their gardens, hothouses, parks and nurseries. To the other less horticultural but equally important individuals and organistions the same measure of gratitude is due.

John Batchelor; Mr and Mrs P. C. Bevis; The Staff of the Language & Literature Department, Birmingham Reference Library; J. L. Blonstein; John Brooks; Margaret Brooks; David and Michelle Broom; Mrs Muriel M. Brown; The Director of the Cambridge University Botanic Garden, and special help from the Assistant Taxonomist C. J. King and Glasshouse Superintendent Sidney Glover; St. Catherine's Church, Wimborne; Robert Cave; Peter Chappell; Beth Chatto; Mr and Mrs Stanley Cherry; Mr T. Chissell; Mr and Mrs K. Coates; Miss H. Coles; Mr G. Colles; Sir Robert and Lady Cooke; Patricia Copson; Richard Cutler; Col. A. R. E. Davis, Lodge Nurseries, Hampreston; Eve Dennis; Barbara Everard; Dr Levi Fox; Bill and Liz Fursdon; Noel Geach; Mrs F. M. Gillard; Colin Graham; Pat Halliday; Sir Michael and Lady Hanham; Mrs M. Harman; Nicholas J. Herbert; Martin Hibbs; Tim and Barbara Hooker; Mr S. F. James; Jardin des Plantes, Paris; Mr and Mrs H. Larkin; Royal Botanic Garden, Kew; Rodney Legge; The Head Librarian and Staff at the Lindley Library; C. J. Marchant, Keeper's Hill Nursery, Stapehill, Dorset; Rosemary McDonald; Mr Victor Montague; Marianne Moores of 'Marianne's'; Dr Goetz Niederau; Virginia Nightingale; Alan Paterson of the Chelsea Physic Garden; Oleg Polunin; Poole Amenities and Recreation Department; Mrs W. E. Powell; Roger W. Pring; Kathleen Rastall; Rosina Nurseries, Ferndown; The Marchioness of Salisbury; Mr and Mrs B. V. Scarborough, 'Naturescape', Colston Bassett, Nottingham; Lord Skelmersdale, Broadleigh Gardens, Somerset; Mr L. Rainsford Smith; Harry Spencer; John Naylor Spensley; Richard and Susan Sweatland; Sally Valentine; Stanley and Margaret Walker; Michael Wallis, Scotts Nurseries, Somerset; Mr and Mrs J. Watson; Mrs K. West; The Chief Librarian and Staff at Wimborne Library.

I want to make a special acknowledgement to my secretary, Rosemary Orr, who made endless lists and vital reminders, typed and retyped the manuscript, and who entered into all the careful research, note-taking and most essential filing with cheerful and conscientious thoroughness and undiminished enthusiasm from the birth of the idea to the last of the proof-reading, and who never once grumbled at my using her typewriter and continually altering all the settings. Without her continuous support throughout this book would not have been such a pleasure to produce, and I thank her.

Introduction

THIS book and its illustrations are a tribute to the greatest of all playwrights. William Shakespeare was born and brought up in the small country town of Stratford-upon-Avon, and throughout his works he used his own close observations of things natural with such mastery that he has forever linked his lines to the same discoveries that each of us can make today – if the eyes of our minds are open. Shakespeare the countryman and poet would have watched and remembered that brief half-bright period of the summer dawn when the rising sun 'fires the proud tops of the eastern pines'[1]. Fortunately for posterity that gilded moment was set down on paper.

Whether his imaginary scenes were set in the Forest of Arden, a wood near Athens, a wild heath in Scotland or a river-bank in Denmark, they were as accurate then as now. This is shown by the lines 'the camomile, the more it is trodden on the faster it grows'[2], and in his description of Prince Hal's wildness, which 'Grew like the summer grass, fastest by night, Unseen yet crescive in his faculty'[3]. This accuracy was often combined with simile, as in 'the female ivy so Enrings the barky fingers of the elm'[4] where the bewitched Titania likens herself to the entwining ivy when she clasps Bottom in her arms.

Shakespeare coloured his descriptions of the seasons with the blossoms and even the vegetables exactly as they would have appeared, and even when whole groups of plants are named they are still in their seasonal flowering or fruiting order. Shakespeare's sensory imagery is illuminated the more brightly by this knowledge. Actual pain is conveyed in Ariel's words: 'Tooth'd briars, sharp furzes, pricking goss, and thorns'[5]; extremes of scent are illustrated in 'violets dim, But sweeter than the lids of Juno's eyes Or Cytherea's breath'[6] and 'most dear actors, eat no onions or garlic for we are to utter sweet breath'[7]; and the visual aspect is most perfectly described in these lines from Love's Labour's Lost[8];

When daisies pied and violets blue
And Lady-smocks all silver-white
And Cuckoo-buds of yellow hue
Do paint the meadows with delight.

Flowers and plants are employed in various ways as symbols: from Ophelia's 'There's Rosemary, that's for remembrance'[9] to the outward manifestations of Lear's sad descent from majesty and sanity – 'Crown'd with rank fumiter and furrow-weeds, With burdocks, hemlock, nettles, cuckoo-flowers, Darnel . . .'[10].

There are problems for the modern interpreter of Shakespeare's works relating to the names of the flowers and herbs that he knew so well, because there was no system of plant nomenclature in the sixteenth century. Long after Shakespeare's death Carl Linnaeus was born in Sweden in 1707, and it was not until after his lifetime's

[1] Richard II, III. ii. 42
[2] 1 Henry IV, II. iv. 441
[3] Henry V, I. i. 65
[4] A Midsummer Night's Dream, IV. i. 47
[5] The Tempest, IV. i. 180
[6] The Winter's Tale, IV. iv. 120
[7] A Midsummer Night's Dream, IV. ii. 42
[8] Love's Labour's Lost, V. ii. 904
[9] Hamlet, IV. v. 175
[10] King Lear, IV. iv. 3

[xi]

work on the classification of plants into their correct natural order that plant taxonomy took on the almost logical aspect that it now possesses. In those days it was still blurred and indistinct because the same plant often had several common names and sometimes several very similar Latin ones, which varied from place to place and country to country.

The monks of the middle ages had made a start in classifying the Latin names of the religious and medicinal plants that they knew and were interested in, but they knew nothing of the gayer and more wanton flowers that graced the gardens of the nobility. The Holy fathers were of necessity copyists, not pioneers, in this field, and what we would now regard as mistakes were constantly perpetuated. Linnaeus, with his binominal method, ended all this medieval chaos, though it did not happen suddenly. It was a gradual process that began during his lifetime and is still continuing today, with plants still being given new names by the botanists where modern research reveals their true classification. Shakespeare's names for some of his plants are thus very different from those of today because they were the common names of his period.

In the bustling, bawdy, lustily expanding England of the sixteenth century, there was a great love of flowers and a respect for plants, which were put to much more use than they are today. That stately and improbable plant, the Crown Imperial, *Fritillaria imperialis*, would have been grown as a very recent importation in the notable gardens of the day, probably including Shakespeare's own at New Place where it still grows today. This strange and exotic-looking flower is easily recognisable among the representations of medicinal plants in early herbals and was grown more for its religious significance than for any supposed medicinal properties.

There are two contemporary sources that have been of considerable help to me in the interpreting of Shakespeare's works. The first was that great gardener, herbalist and 'chirurgeon' John Gerard, who lived in Shakespeare's time and who was responsible for several famous gardens of the time as well as his own, where he grew 'over 1000 sorts'. Gerard loved his plants and in 1596 triumphantly listed those rarities that he had persuaded to grow despite the inclemencies of the English climate. Many of them were imported from the far and middle East, via Holland, and how they must have shivered in the cold soil of his London garden, notwithstanding the most excellent care that he could contrive for them. 'I have them in my garden' he says, again and again in his own writings. Gerard's plant list was the first of its kind and it is lodged in the British Museum. According to the standards of his time, the old herbalist was most knowledgeable in the history and superstitions attaching to all his vegetable treasures, and it is quite probable that he would have passed on to Shakespeare much that he knew of his latest acquisitions. The second source was William Turner, who lived from *c.* 1508 to 1579 and who produced several scholarly works on plants and herbs: the most famous of them, the *Herbal*, was published in three parts in 1551, 1562 and 1568.

Despite this very valuable material which related specifically to the plants and gardens of the sixteenth century, there are some names that Shakespeare used which are forever beyond precise definition. For instance, 'Long Purples', 'Hebona', 'Spear-grass', 'Flower-de-Luce' and 'Lark's-Heels' are some of the teasing plant-names which may never be satisfactorily explained. For me, this lends fascination and mystery to the incomparable verses.

> *. . . daffodils,*
> *That come before the swallow dares, and take*
> *The winds of March with beauty; violets dim,*
> *But sweeter than the lids of Juno's eyes*
> *Or Cytherea's breath; pale primroses,*
> *That die unmarried, ere they can behold*
> *Bright Phoebus in his strength,*
> Perdita – *The Winter's Tale*, IV, iv. 118

1 DAFFODIL
Narcissus pseudo-narcissus

In *The Winter's Tale*, Shakespeare employed the pastoral convention, a literary device which used the idyllic life of shepherds as a setting. Here floral description and invocation of classical goddesses evoke a mood of unity with nature.

The Daffodil that Shakespeare knew best is the Wild Daffodil native to the woodlands of England, where it once grew in abundance; now the delicate papery-pale flowers are rarely seen unless they have been re-introduced. It is known from plant-lists of the time that over twenty new varieties of the flower had been brought to England from Europe or even further eastwards.

2 VIOLET
Viola odorata

Shakespeare makes many references to the purple sweet-scented Violet in his works. Before his time, the name 'Violet' was loosely given to many different spring flowers, such as the Snowdrop (*Galanthus nivalis*) which was called 'Viola alba' in 1542. At that time, Honesty (*Lunaria biennis*) was called 'Viola Lunaria major', and the Canterbury Bell (*Campanula medium*), whatever its colour, was known as 'Viola Mariana'. By his constant reference to the flower, Shakespeare determined the name for posterity long before the lifetime of the great Linnaeus.

3 PRIMROSE
Primula vulgaris

Primroses are a unique shade of pale greenish yellow – the colour of watery spring sunlight.

The name 'Primrose' is derived from the Italian *flor di prima vera* ('flower of spring'). This was shortened to *primerole*, then to *primerolles*, which finally became our much-loved 'Primrose'.

It should be remembered that the Primrose is now a protected plant in the United Kingdom.

Witness this primrose bank whereon I lie;
Venus and Adonis 151

. . . nor
The azured harebell, like thy veins;
Arviragus – *Cymbeline*, IV. ii. 221

Kate like the hazel-twig
Is straight and slender, and as brown in hue
Petruchio – *The Taming of the Shrew*, II. i. 255

1 PRIMROSE
primula vulgaris

A mossy lawn with old fruit-trees is one of the best nurseries for Primrose seedlings. If mature clumps of Primroses are planted beneath the trees and allowed to flower and set seed, the following year minute seedlings, with the recognisable crinkled leaf, should have appeared in the mossy grass. Moss in the lawn is an indication of dampness and the seedlings will do best in this very natural environment. The little plants should be allowed to grow on throughout the summer, and should flower in the following spring.

2 HAREBELL
(Bluebell)
Endymion non-scriptus

The illustration shows the English Bluebell. It is generally considered that Shakespeare was thinking of this flower, because it blooms with the Primrose (which is also mentioned in this speech), whereas the Harebell (*Campanula rotundifolia*), which is called 'Bluebell' in Scotland, flowers much later in the year (from July to September). The Bluebell's Latin name is taken from the Greek legend of the beautiful youth Hyacinthus who was beloved by Apollo the Sun-god, and Zephyrus, God of the West Wind. In a game of quoits Hyacinthus was deliberately killed by the jealous Zephyrus. The grief-stricken Apollo caused a beautiful blue flower to spring up from the blood-soaked ground; this Greek variety of the flower was marked with the Greek symbol for 'woe' and, ever after, the Northern European Bluebell was called *Endymion non-scriptus* – 'not written upon'.

3 HAZEL
Corylus avellana

Hazel twigs have always been associated with 'dowsing' or water-divining, and this strangely magical gift sleeps unawakened in many of us. A freshly-cut forked twig of Hazel is used, and this is held with the forked ends in each hand. The water-diviner walks to and fro over the chosen area, and if there is natural water beneath the twig will move strongly downwards of its own accord. This strange ability, present in some and not in others, has never been satisfactorily explained.

2

3

1

> *. . . for look here what I found*
> *on a palm tree.*
> Rosalind – *As You Like It*, III. ii. 185

> *. . . to take note how many pair of silk*
> *stockings thou hast, viz. these, and those that*
> *were thy peach-coloured ones!*
> Prince Hal – *2 Henry IV*, II. ii. 17

1 PALM
(Sallow)
Salix caprea

There are several passages in the plays which mention Palm, and it is clear that two very different Palm trees are intended. In the quotation above (where Orlando has hung the trees of the Forest of Arden with his verses addressed to the tart-tongued Rosalind) it is the variety of Willow commonly called 'Pussy Willow' by English children that is meant. The branches of this tree are used on Palm Sunday to decorate churches, though it is not known why this very dissimilar tree was substituted for the traditional Palm that is pictured in scriptural illustration (See Date Palm, p. 136.) Why this tree of all others should be used has never been adequately explained, though there is a Biblical direction (Leviticus XXIII: 40) about the preparation for the feast of the Tabernacles which says: 'Ye shall take you on the first day the boughs of goodly trees, and branches of palm trees, and the boughs of thick trees, and willows from the brook . . .' and it may be that there was an association of ideas; certainly there are Church records of similar trees being planted in or near churchyards in the eighteenth century.

2 PEACH
Prunus persica

Peaches really need the protection of a glasshouse to give of their best in the British Isles, except in mild winters in Devon, Cornwall and the Isles of Scilly.

The fruiting tree was known in this country as early as the tenth century, and many ecclesiastical records show payments made to gardeners for the especial care needed for the Peach-trees. The trees will grow very quickly and easily, even from a Peach-stone sown in a pot, and will begin to flower in February from about the fifth year. The flowers are always bright sugar-pink, but even in a sheltered garden the sudden frosts or heavy rains of early spring can damage the blossom badly. Though the trees are self-fertilising, it is better if Peach trees of a different variety are planted nearby. February is usually too early for hive bees to act as pollinators, so pollination by hand should be done, using a soft camel-hair paint-brush at midday, every day while the flowers last. Peach trees are subject to a considerable number of pests and diseases, and their cultivation demands great care and attention.

1

2

1

> *Emilia:*   *This garden has a world of pleasures in't*
> *What flower is this?*
> *Woman:*   *'Tis called Narcissus, madam.*
> *Emilia:*   *That was a fair boy, certain, but a fool*
> *To love himself. Were there not maids enough?*
> *The Two Noble Kinsmen,* II. ii. 118

NARCISSUS
Narcissus poeticus
'Actaea'

Emilia is talking of the legend of the beautiful boy Narcissus, son of the river-god Cephisus. Narcissus scorned the affections of the river nymphs, being incapable of love for any woman. Echo was the most beautiful of the nymphs and, like many beautiful women, was accustomed to having her own way. Piqued by the rejection of her love, she caused him to fall in love with his own reflection, seen in a pool of the river. Narcissus pined with longing for this beautiful youth, and, as he pined away, so he changed into a flower. The word 'narcissism' has thus come to mean an extreme of vanity.

Before Shakespeare's time, many kinds of Narcissus and Daffodil (for they are of the same family) had been brought to England and these were grown in the great gardens of the times. Gerard and Turner knew of them, and John Parkinson attempted to catalogue the varieties then known, and in his great book *Paradisus Terrestris* (1629) he was able to list some 96 varieties.

Narcissus poeticus ('Poet's Narcissus') is still found in the wild in the mountainous regions from Spain to Greece. There are many named varieties.

Yon little tree, yon blooming apricock;
Palamon – *The Two Noble Kinsmen*, II. ii. 239

. . . wearing on their heads
garlands of bays . . .
The Vision – *Henry VIII*, IV. ii. 82

. . . the parrot
will not do more for an almond . . .
Thersites – *Troilus and Cressida*, V. ii. 193

1 APRICOCK
(Apricot)
Prunus armeniaca

The Apricot, or Apricock, acquired its name in Shakespeare's time because it flowered and fruited earliest of all the fruit trees. Lyte commented in 1578 on a kind of Peach called 'Abrecox' or 'Aprecox', which is derived from the Latin *praecox* meaning 'precocious' or 'ripe before its time'. It is interesting to note that the summers in Tudor England must indeed have been much warmer in order to ripen these golden fruits so often associated with Mediterranean lands, though the Apricot was originally brought from China.

2 BAY
Laurus nobilis

The Bay of noble legend is often confused with the Laurel (see page 122). The 'sweet' Bay is a true Laurel botanically, but the distinctions between the species were not known until the time of Carl Linnaeus. The Bay has been called the victor's Laurel, because ceremonial wreaths and garlands were made of it to honour victorious generals who brought their armies safely back. Poets were crowned with (Laurel) wreaths made of the sweet Bay, and the term 'Poet Laureate' originated from the custom of honouring the successors to that title with a dignified wreath of the leaves. The Bay does not always flower in the British Isles, and the leaves are often shrivelled and browned by the cold winds of winter, but with the warmth of spring and early summer the bush (or tree) will re-clothe itself in fresh young leaves which will darken by late summer to the familiar sombre dark green.

3 ALMOND
Prunus dulcis

It is possible that there was an old proverb 'An Almond for a parrot' which meant the highest temptation for a man, and this is probably the root of this line from Shakespeare. Almond trees are particularly distinctive in early spring, when the bare branches are tipped with muffs of clear sugar-pink. The kernels of the sweet Almond have been used in the confectionery trade for thousands of years, and a favourite Elizabethan sweetmeat was 'marchpane', almost the same as our present-day marzipan. Until quite recently the kernels of Peaches were mixed with those of Almonds, and the adulterated paste sold for the same high price as pure ground Almonds.

I prithee, let me bring thee where crabs grow;
And I with my long nails will dig thee pig-nuts;
. . . I'll bring thee
To clustering filberts, and sometimes I'll get thee
Young scamels from the rock. Wilt thou go with me?
Caliban – *The Tempest*, II. ii. 171

The rank of osiers by the murmuring stream
Left on your right hand brings you to the place.
Celia – *As You Like It*, IV. iii. 80

1 CRAB-APPLE
Malus var. 'Profusion'
1a Malus sylvestris

Shakespeare mentions many kinds of Apple (see p. 32), but here he is speaking of the wild Crab-apple, *Malus sylvestris* (1a), which was much more commonly grown for its fruit in the sixteenth century than it is today. Strangely, this was not because there were not better and larger apples then, but because the taste of the 'Crabs' was often preferred, particularly when roasted and dropped into hot ale. Today's ornamental 'Crabs', are mainly grown for the beauty of their flowers and the illustration also shows one of these.

2 PIGNUT
Conopodium majus

Pignuts are impossible to find unless the flowering stem still remains above as a guide. The 'nut' or tuber may be at least six inches below ground, among the crowding roots of the trees, and it is hard work to trace the delicate stem down through these to get at the small round tuber, but well worth the trouble and effort – Pignuts are a forgotten country tit-bit. The flowers are found in open woodland, often in company with Bluebells, Primroses and Dog's Mercury.

3 FILBERT
Corylus maxima

Filbert catkins in a mild winter will be longer than those of the Hazel, but if the frosts are hard and persistent the catkins will not mature. The Filbert (Christianised by being named after St Philibert) differs from the Hazel by having larger leaves and being altogether stouter in its appearance.

All the woodland wildlife will begin to anticipate the nut-harvest from late summer onwards; too early and the nuts are green and tasteless, too late and they have all vanished, except for a rejected few which are greyish-brown in colour. These are the discards that the animals and birds have avoided because the kernels have turned to dust.

4 OSIER
Salix viminalis

Osier is a locally common name for the species of Willow that was formerly grown for basket-making. The Osiers, which were the long thin 'canes', were cultivated in marshy areas that were conducive to quick top-growth, and the 'Osiers' would grow as much as ten to twelve feet in a single season, a useful commercial length.

2

4

3

1

1a

The even mead, that erst brought sweetly forth
The freckled cowslip, burnet and green clover,
Duke of Burgundy – *Henry V*, V. ii. 48

A purple flower sprung up, chequer'd with white,
Venus and Adonis 1168

1 COWSLIP
Primula veris

Shakespeare likened the Cowslip, in the line from *A Midsummer Night's Dream* 'The cowslips tall her pensioners be;' to Queen Elizabeth I's 'pensioners', who were fifty tall and handsome young men of noble birth. These privileged youths were dressed in golden livery, and proudly wore the Queen's 'favours' which might have been a ruby or other precious jewel.

2 BURNET
Poterium sanguisorba

The delicate-leaved Burnet often grows in the same fields as the Cowslip, and flowers at the same time. In Shakespeare's day, many salads (or 'sallets') were eaten, and many wild plants were regularly gathered to supply this need. Burnet smells of Cucumber when crushed, and it was one of the known salad herbs of that time.

3 CLOVER
Trifolium repens, Trifolium pratense

All the clovers begin to flower at Cowslip-time, making a feast of nectar for the winter-hungry bees.

Red Clover was used medicinally in the middle ages, and several English place-names like Claverton in Somerset, Claverley in Shropshire, Claverdon in Warwickshire and Clavering in Essex are derived from the Old English word *Clāfre*.

Fortunate is the person who finds a four-leaved Clover, because such a find is said to mean the granting of a wish and the power to see the little people dancing the night away in their fairy rings.

4 SNAKE'S HEAD FRITILLARY
Fritillaria meleagris

Most other interpreters of this quotation state that the flower intended (but not actually named by Shakespeare) was the Wood Anemone, *Anemone nemorosa*, because it was the only flower they knew of which remotely fitted the description. The logical and seldom-considered candidate for the title of Shakespeare's 'chequer'd flower', however, is the Snake's Head Fritillary, being the only 'chequered' wild flower in the British Isles. This curiously beautiful flower was first brought to England in 1557 by an apothecary called Noel Caperon, who found it growing wild near Orleans in France. Gerard and Lyte both grew it in their gardens. This strangely-coloured flower is so named because its buds look like the head of a striking snake.

There with fantastic garlands did she come
Of crow-flowers, nettles, daisies, and long purples,
That liberal shepherds give a grosser name,
But our cold maids do dead men's fingers call them:
Gertrude – *Hamlet*, IV. vii. 169

1 CROWFLOWER
(Ragged Robin)
Lychnis flos-cuculi

The name 'Crowflower' has been the subject of some disagreement, but in Shakespeare's time it referred to Ragged Robin. The great herbalist and gardener Gerard, who was a contemporary, said of these flowers that they were 'used for garlands and crowns'.

Ragged Robin grows only in damp meadows, ditches and by the waterside, so it is a logical thought, if logic could ever apply to poor, sad, mad Ophelia, that she would have caught up whatever came to hand to make her chaplet.

2 NETTLES
(White Deadnettle)
Lamium album

It is unlikely that the garlands of the quotation included stinging nettles but the White Deadnettle does not sting, and might therefore have been chosen. It, too, grows in the same damp situations in the early summer. This is a flower that is so common a sight in hedgebanks that it is often ignored. Nevertheless it is a very interesting plant. Pick a flower stem and turn it upside-down and the reason for one of its old folk-names will be seen – there they are, 'Adam and Eve in a Bower', cosily nestling together and shaded from prying eyes by the green-white hood of the flower.

3 DAISY
(Ox-eye Daisy, Moon-Daisy, Dog-Daisy)
Chrysanthemum leucanthemum

This daisy's stiff wiry stems make it a difficult flower to pick. Though it is a wild flower of meadows and hedgebanks, it looks like a Marguerite in miniature (which indeed it is).

4 LONG PURPLES
(Early Purple Orchid)
Orchis mascula
5 LONG PURPLES
(Cuckoo-Pint, Lords and Ladies, Wake-Robin, Jack-in-the Pulpit, etc)
Arum maculatum

The two plants have many shared local names, most of them explicitly sexual. Both flower at the same time, both like a damp habitat, and both usually have spotted leaves. *Orchis mascula* has two tubers at the base of the flower-stalk, which together with the upright stem have a particularly physical connotation. The Cuckoo-Pint is a plant of many names, and because of its blatantly phallic appearance there are many superstitions about its magical power to improve or retard sexual potency.

The question of what flowers comprised Ophelia's 'Long Purples' will be argued over for all time. The plate illustrates both flowers.

4

2

3

5

1

When daisies pied and violets blue
  And lady-smocks all silver-white
And cuckoo-buds of yellow hue
  Do paint the meadows with delight,
    Armado – *Love's Labour's Lost*, V. ii. 904

1 DAISY
Bellis perennis

In the British Isles a mild winter means that Daisies can be found in flower all year round. Nevertheless, Daisies were traditionally regarded as the heralds of spring and summer. There is an old saying: 'When you can put your foot on seven Daisies, summer is come.'

To most people, Daisies of one type or another are a symbol of freshness, purity and simplicity.

2 VIOLET
(Woodland Violet, Dog Violet)
Viola riviniana

This wild Violet is scentless, but makes up for this by flowering in such profusion on grassy banks, meadows and at the edges of open woods that the short grass is a haze of blue-mauve. Any flower-name prefixed by the word 'Dog' meant that the plant in question was of an inferior type, and usually without scent. This may be seen when this violet is compared to *Viola odorata* which has flowers of amethyst-purple and a legendary perfume.

3 LADY-SMOCK
(Cuckoo-flower)
Cardamine pratensis

Many English plant-names are derived from Scandinavian or Central European folk-lore or from classical mythology. The derivation of the name 'Cuckoo-flower' can be traced to the fact that the plant flowers when the cuckoo begins to call in the spring. This means that it is an unlucky flower usually associated with the devil. Flower-names that begin with the word 'Lady', however, date from the early Middle ages, and indicate an association with the Virgin Mary (her attributes, appearance or attire). Many flower-names were afterwards Christianised in this way in an attempt to avert ill luck; another example of this is Lady's Fingers, once called 'Cuckoo's Stockings', but more commonly known today as Bird's-foot Trefoil, *Lotus corniculatus*.

4 CUCKOO-BUDS
(Meadow Buttercup)
Ranunculus acris

It is assumed by most people, because of the association of the other three flowers in the quotation, that the 'Cuckoo-buds' are the graceful Buttercups of English meadows.

. . . those lily hands
Tremble, like aspen-leaves, upon a lute,
Marcus – *Titus Andronicus*, II. iv. 44

How like Eve's apple doth thy beauty grow,
Sonnet XCIII

I stamp this kiss upon thy currant lip;
Thesius – *The Two Noble Kinsmen*, I. i. 216

1 LILY-OF-THE-
VALLEY
Convallaria majalis

The sweetly powerful scent and pure whiteness of this cottage-garden flower are familiar to all gardeners. Lilies-of-the-valley are quite hardy, and thrive best in a semi-shaded position that is not too dry. The plants will do even better if they are grown in light woodland conditions. The occasional berries that are produced are very poisonous, but can be dried and planted to increase the stock.

2 ASPEN
Populus tremula

Aspens have always been described as quaking, shivering or trembling, and this is because the long leaf petiole is compressed laterally, which causes the constant movement of the leaves, even when there appears to be no breeze whatsoever. Legends about the Aspen were many, and its miserable shivering was said to be because Christ was crucified on a cross of Aspen-wood. In the middle ages country people hated and feared Aspen trees, and would often throw stones and clods of earth at them.

3 APPLE
Malus domestica

Shakespeare names seven types of Apple: the Codling, the Pomewater, the Bitter-Sweeting, the Leathercoat, the Pippin, the Apple-john and the Crab-apple (see p. 24). Apples were valued for their keeping qualities more in those days, and it is thought that the Apple-john was a particularly long-lasting variety called in Victorian times the 'Easter Pippin' because it lasted through the winter. Pippins were Apple trees grown from pips rather than grafts; Leathercoats were russets; the Bitter-Sweeting was probably a form of cider apple; the Pomewater was thought by Parkinson to be similar to a variety called Lord Suffield; and Codlings were unripe apples.

4 RED CURRANT
Ribes rubrum

Currants, in particular the red variety, were just beginning to be cultivated from the wild in Shakespeare's time, and Gerard describes them as newly growing in his great garden in London.

Where fires thou find'st unraked and hearths unswept,
There pinch the maids as blue as bilberry:
Pistol – *The Merry Wives of Windsor*, V. v. 48

. . . I warrant they would whip
me with their fine wits till I were as crest-fallen
as a dried pear.
Falstaff – *The Merry Wives of Windsor*, IV. v. 101

Now, as fond fathers,
Having bound up the threatening twigs of birch,
Vincentio – *Measure for Measure*, I. iii. 23

Quince   Dramatis persona, A Midsummer Night's Dream

1 BILBERRY,
BLUEBERRY,
HUCKLEBERRY
Vaccinium myrtillus

Wild Bilberries grow on the high damp moors of the British Isles and their small ripe fruit makes a delicious pie filling. Teeth and tongue are temporarily stained by the juice as blue as the woad of the ancient Britons, and so are the hands that pick the fruit.

2 PEAR
Pyrus communis

There were very many types of Pear in Tudor times, but Shakespeare names only two of them in his works – the Warden and the Poperin. The flowers are always snow-white, and an old Pear-tree in blossom is a fine sight, even if the tree no longer yields much fruit. Sometimes this is because there is no longer a similar Pear in the immediate vicinity for cross-pollination.

3 BIRCH
Betula pendula

Of all trees in winter, a leafless Birch is one of the most graceful, with its hanging curtains of delicate branches and its peeling black and silver bark. Sometimes in the autumn all the leaves turn yellow simultaneously, and the tree, if seen in isolation against a dark background, will look like a golden candle-flame.

4 QUINCE
Cydonia oblonga

Quinces were grown more often in Shakespeare's time, and before then the Romans regarded the fruits as love-tokens. They would give them as gifts, throw them at each other, and ceremonially eat them together; even dreaming of Quinces was an indication of success in love.

1

2

4

3

Elinor: *Come to thy grandam, child.*
Constance: *Do, child, go to it grandam, child;*
              Give grandam kingdom, and it grandam will
              Give it a plum, a cherry, and a fig:
                              King John, II, i. 160

Feed him with apricocks and dewberries,
          Titania – *A Midsummer Night's Dream*, III. i. 169

1 PLUM
Prunus domestica

There were almost as many known varieties of Plum in Shakespeare's time as there are today. Gerard could count 'threescore sorts' in his garden, which were all 'strange and rare'; and more were being discovered each year.

2 CHERRY
Prunus avium

Cherries are one of the jewels of the vegetable world, but the sweet Cherry is not always an easy tree to grow. It needs plenty of rain in the summer months, sun at the right time to ripen and colour the fruit, and it will not tolerate too much frost. It is thought that the Romans introduced the first Cherry trees into the British Isles.

3 FIG
Ficus carica

Figs are strange trees in that the flowers are totally concealed within the growing 'fruit'. The outer skin encloses a number of flowers which grow to perfect maturity and ripen their seeds in complete darkness.

4 APRICOCK
(Apricot)
Prunus armeniaca

Apricots are grown in France and the Mediterranean countries. Apricot oil, which is made from the kernels, is used extensively in the cosmetic industry because it has a gentle and softening effect on the skin.

5 DEWBERRY
Rubus caesius

Dewberries look like smaller, simpler Blackberries, with fewer 'drupes' which have a bluish bloom and a distinctive flavour. The bushes are never as large as those of the Blackberry, and the leaves are paler green.

. . . bold oxlips and
The crown-imperial;
Perdita – *The Winter's Tale*, IV. iv. 125

1 OXLIP
Primula elatior

True Oxlips are a rare wild flower in the British Isles, found
naturally growing in only a few Eastern counties. The flowers are
distinguished from their variable cousin the False Oxlip (which is a
cross between the Cowslip and the Primrose) by the orange spots at
the base of the petals, the sweet apricot scent and by the one-sided
habit of the flower-scape. If seeds of the true Oxlip are grown, the
tiny plants will not flower in their first year, and may not in the
second. However, they will put on much leafy growth, and in the
third year the pale yellow flowers will appear. Oxlips should be
planted as far away as possible from any Primroses in the same
garden, or curious hybrids will appear because of cross-pollination;
true Oxlips prefer semi-shade and woodland conditions, whereas the
false variety likes the sunny situation of its Cowslip parent.

2 CROWN
IMPERIAL
Fritillaria imperialis

These astonishing flowers look curiously tropical and out of place in
an English garden in March. They were brought to England from
the Himalayas via Persia in the early part of the sixteenth century,
and they were very popular in the great gardens of Tudor England.

Fortunately this plant has, in a way, stood still in time, and has not
been hybridised out of all recognition. There are still two varieties
that are commonly grown: *lutea*, which is yellow, and *rubra*, which is
burnt-orange in colour and is illustrated here.

The flowers come very early in the year for such an exotic, summer-
seeming plant, and smell most powerfully of fox.

Legend says that the lily-like flowers of the Crown Imperial were
once white and pointed upwards, and that they grew in the garden
of Gethsemane among many other beautiful flowers. As Our Lord
walked sadly past them, the flowers bowed their heads in sympathy
– all but the Crown Imperial, proud and haughty because of its own
crown of leaves. Christ noticed this one conceited plant and turned
back and rebuked it, and at once it hung its head in shame and
blushed crimson, and tears appeared in its eyes. These 'tears' are
drops of nectar that hang within the flower-bells still, and they
cannot be dislodged even if the flower-head is shaken vigorously.
The huge bulbs should be planted on their sides eight inches deep
on a bed of sharp sand or grit. The flowers will come up year after
year and the bulbs should not be disturbed.

2

I

Grew like the summer grass, fastest by night,
Unseen, yet crescive in his faculty.
                    Bishop of Ely – *Henry V*, I. i. 65

With words more sweet, and yet more dangerous,
Than baits to fish, or honey-stalks to sheep;
                    Tamora – *Titus Andronicus*, IV. iv. 90

Thy turfy mountains, where live nibbling sheep,
And flat meads thatch'd with stover, them to keep;
                    Iris – *The Tempest*, IV. i. 62

Grass
1 YORKSHIRE FOG
Holcus lanatus
2 COCKSFOOT
Dactylis glomerata
3 TALL OAT
GRASS
Arrhenatherum elatius

Grass in general is taken for granted all over the world except in the region of the polar ice-caps. However, a single blade of grass is powerful enough to grow up through man's abandoned concrete wastes, and grass is the only plant that will keep whole areas of desert dunes from their restless march, anchoring them down with a net of living grass-roots that is often the beginning of great conservation programmes. After the grass has become established other small plants will begin to seed themselves and after these will come the shrubs and trees. In former times, grass constituted nine-tenths of the vegetation of the world.

Honey-stalk
4 RED CLOVER
Trifolium pratense
5 WHITE CLOVER
Trifolium repens

It is believed that Shakespeare meant the flowers of Clover by the term 'Honey-stalks' in this quotation because the tubular Clover-flowers are so rich in honey. Sheep will over-eat in a field of clover if they get the chance, and the lush spring growth of clover is the most dangerous for them. A certain amount of Clover is an excellent thing, for the ewes early in the year, but Tamora's allusion to the dangers of Honey-stalks to sheep meant that such over-eating could be fatal.

STOVER
(Hay, Dried Grass, Straw)

The word 'Stover' was much used in medieval times to mean hay, straw, or late pasturage in the fields. The word is derived originally from the Old French *Estover* ('to be necessary'), and this word later became a legal term, meaning certain kinds of maintenance.

. . . so I charm'd their ears,
That, calf-like, they my lowing follow'd through
Tooth'd briers, sharp furzes, pricking goss, and thorns,
Which enter'd their frail shins:
                    Ariel – *The Tempest*, IV. i. 178

1 BRIAR
Rubus species

There is an old story told about the Briar, or Bramble, and a cormorant. This cormorant was a wool merchant, who entered into a partnership with the bramble and a bat to provide a large ship with a cargo of wool. The ship was wrecked, and the three became bankrupt. Since then, the bat flies only at dusk to avoid his creditors, the cormorant dives forever into the sea to search for their sunken ship, and the briar plucks wool from every passing sheep in an effort to make up the loss from the stolen wool.

2 FURZE, GOSS
(Gorse)
Ulex europaeus

It is unlikely that in the sixteenth century the two more common types of Gorse, Goss, or Furze would have been separately identified. *Ulex europaeus* is the larger plant, and this is the one that covers whole hillsides with sheets of scented golden flowers in early summer. *Ulex gallii* is smaller, and begins to flower from July onwards.

3 THORN
BLACKTHORN
Prunus spinosa

White flowers on the black branches of the Blackthorn against a blue sky indicate that spring is here and summer just round the corner. The tree itself has been of use to man since earliest times, providing an impenetrable hedge to keep his livestock from straying, blue-bloomed sloes in the autumn to flavour his gin, and everlasting stout walking-sticks to support him in his own old age. Both flowers and fruit (sloes) are illustrated (3a).

1

3

3a

2

The count is neither sad, nor sick, nor
merry, nor well; but civil count, civil as an
orange, and something of that jealous complexion.
Beatrice – *Much Ado About Nothing*, II. i. 303

. . . let them say of me, 'As jealous as Ford, that
searched a hollow walnut for his wife's leman.'
Ford – *The Merry Wives of Windsor*, IV. ii. 170

. . . all the other gifts appertinent
to man, as the malice of this age shapes them, are
not worth a gooseberry.
Falstaff – *2 Henry IV*, I. ii. 194

1 and 1a ORANGE
Citrus aurantium

There are documented records of orange trees first being grown in the British Isles in 1578. It was recognised that these trees of warmer lands needed to be protected in winter, and the special buildings that were erected then would have been the forerunners of the magnificent Orangeries that were later to be built in Northern Europe. The illustration shows the flowers and fruit of *Citrus sinensis* which can be grown as a house-plant; the tiny oranges are juicy but sour, and they are excellent for marmalade-making.

2 WALNUT
Juglans regia

In Shakespeare's time full-grown Walnut trees, which are not native to the British Isles, were nevertheless well known; to attain this maturity they would have to have been planted many hundreds of years before he was born. There is a record in the *Gardener's Chronicle* of a very ancient tree that was reputed to be over 1,000 years old; this Walnut tree was still bearing an annual crop of thousands of nuts in the later part of the nineteenth century. The Walnut is a great and beautiful tree, with its fissured trunk and graceful leaf-sprays, and it is valued by furniture craftsmen for the grain of the timber, by gunsmiths for the wood for gunstocks, and by artists for the purity of the distilled oil which is used in the manufacture of paints. The huge harvests of nuts are appreciated by man and squirrel alike, and the carefully-dried leaves are still used for homoeopathic remedies.

3 GOOSEBERRY
Ribes uva-crispa

The name 'Gooseberry' has nothing to do with geese, but is a probable corruption of the word 'Crossberry'. During the times of the Plagues patients were recommended to eat Gooseberries, which were also known as 'Feaberries' or 'Thepes'.

2

1 a

3

1

*This green plot shall
be our stage, this hawthorn-brake our tiring-
house;*
> Quince – *A Midsummer-Night's Dream*, III. i. 3

Get ye all three into the box-tree:
> Maria – *Twelfth Night*, II. v. 18

Dogberry   Dramatis persona, Much Ado About Nothing

1 HAWTHORN
Crataegus monogyna

The Hawthorn of England is a tree of great antiquity and magical associations, and in this famous play about fairies it is fitting that this 'fairy tree' is used as a setting. In medieval England the Hawthorn (or May) was a most important part of the St. John's Eve and Mayday celebrations, which were a pagan fertility festival. Flowering branches of the Hawthorn were brought in from the fields at dawn on Mayday (never earlier) and woven into garlands for the maypole, already set up in readiness on many a village green.

More protection was necessary at this time than at any other against the busy witches and bad fairies who would blight the crops, sour the milk, and do all kinds of mischief like exchanging a mortal child for one of their own dark changelings. Appropriate flowers and leaves were gathered at the proper time, and the correct spells were said and sung to keep all safe for another year.

2 BOX
Buxus sempervirens

Hundreds of years ago, full-size Box trees were common in England. There are few left now, except in one historic area, Box Hill, in the county of Surrey. Box was beloved by the Victorians because it was slow-growing, long-lasting and could be clipped and trained into all kinds of tortuous forms of topiary work, from the neat severity of a herb-bed hedge to a life-sized set of chessmen.

3 DOGBERRY
(Dogwood)
Thelycrania sanguinea

A decoction of Dogwood was formerly used to wash mangy dogs – hence the name. The autumn leaves of crimson-purple are a wonderful colour in the country hedgerow, as are the winter stems of this plant which turn to brilliant crimson in January. (The illustration shows the autumn colouration of the leaves).

Thy banks with pioned and twilled brims,
Which spongy April at they hest betrims,
To make cold nymphs chaste crowns;
Iris – *The Tempest*, IV. i. 64

PIONY
(Peony or Paeony)
Paeonia officinalis

There is an academic dispute about whether Shakespeare intended the word 'pioned' to mean the flower Paeony. In Tudor times the word 'pioner' meant a digger, but this word is now obsolete, surviving only in the word 'pioneer' ('one who goes before'). It is clear that Shakespeare was well aware of this meaning of the word 'pioner' because in *Hamlet* (I. v. 161) there are the lines:

Well said, old mole! canst work i' the earth so fast?
A worthy pioner!

and in *The Rape of Lucrece* (1380):

There might you see the labouring pioner
Begrimed with sweat and smeared all with dust;

Nevertheless, this particular passage from *The Tempest* makes no real sense if the word 'pioned' has a digging connotation; and therefore it seems far more likely that he was referring to the Paeony, which is in bud in April. (It has also been put forward that the Marsh Marigold was the flower intended here, but there is no proof of this.)

The cultivated Paeony has been known in England since the tenth century, and the 'wild' Paeony of Steep Holm island in the Bristol Channel was probably brought from Mediterranean shores by the monks who founded a priory on the island in the eleventh century.

The Paeony is a long-lived plant and there are many established clumps which are over fifty years old. Paeonies resent disturbance and will usually sulk, flowerless, for several years, if moved. They are the most handsome of plants, with great flowers whose colours range from pure white through a range of pinks, salmon and rose to the deep ruby red of the illustration, which is one of the most familiar of all the varieties.

There's rosemary, that's for remembrance:
pray you, love, remember: and there is pansies,
that's for thoughts.
Ophelia – *Hamlet*, IV. v. 175

. . . my wife desired some damsons,
And made me climb, with danger of my life.
Simpcox – *2 Henry VI*, II. i. 102

1 ROSEMARY
Rosmarinus officinalis

An old name for Rosemary was Rosmarin, which means 'the plant that delights in the sea-spray'. Rosemary certainly flowers with more luxuriance along the warm shores of the Mediterranean, and it is not always hardy in the British Isles except on the southern sea coasts. As a perfume it was appreciated much more in Elizabethan times than it is today, and because of its long-lasting and aromatic scent it was nearly always included in the recipes for pot-pourris, pomanders, burning perfumes, scented waters, pillows, sachets and all the many artifices with which the Tudor goodwife attempted to defeat the noisome stenches of those times. Because the scent is so long-lasting and the leaves almost evergreen, Rosemary came to be associated with funerals as a flower of remembrance, and at weddings as a flower of constancy.

2 PANSY
Viola wittrockiana

The English word 'Pansy' is derived from the French *pensée* ('thought'), and Ophelia here alludes to this origin.

The wonderful colours of today's flowers did not exist in Shakespeare's time; these began to make their appearance from France in 1875 and onwards. Pansies are easy to grow and their many 'faces' are very expressive.

3 DAMSON
Prunus insititia

The sharp tang of Damsons is in direct contrast to the insipidity of the late dessert plums; though, of course, a Damson is just a different variety of plum.

Damsons take their name from the city of Damascus, which indicates that they were cultivated and appreciated far more in the middle east in medieval times than they are today.

There's fennel for you, and columbines:
there's rue for you: and here's some for me:
we may call it herb of grace o' Sundays:
Ophelia – *Hamlet*, IV. v. 180

1 FENNEL
Foeniculum vulgare

Fennel was one of the plants listed in fifteenth-century manuscripts as being essential in a garden, which was then a mixture of flowers and herbs, all of which had special 'virtues' in addition to their actual or considered culinary or medicinal value. For example, Fennel was used as a garnish and flavouring for fish, as it still is today, and as it imparts a strong flavour of liquorice in the cooking the fish must have a definite character of its own. In *2 Henry IV*, Shakespeare speaks of eating Conger (eel) and Fennel together; as Fennel was considered to be a herb of venery, and Conger has a particularly powerful flavour, this would have been a most licentious act.

The plant was also emblematical of cajolery or flattery, as the tone of the quotation illustrates.

2 COLUMBINE
Aquilegia vulgaris

The Columbines of the illustration are the very ordinary varieties that seed themselves about so annoyingly to the tidy-minded gardener. The modern long-spurred varieties are very beautiful, but are not as sturdy or as long-lived as these old-fashioned cottage-garden colours. The name Columbine is taken from the Latin *columba* ('dove'), from the likeness of the flower to a circle of pigeons sitting round a dish, which was often portrayed by the artists of those days.

3 RUE
Ruta graveolens
var. 'Jackman's Blue'

Rue is indeed a 'nose-herb' as Lafeu so rightly calls it in *All's Well* (IV. v. 19) and it has always been a herb of sadness and repentence. 'Ruth' was the archaic word for sorrow, remorse, regret and pity, and the verb 'to rue' developed from this root. Rue is bitter to the taste, and therefore it early became particularly associated with repentence. It was also called the 'Herb of Grace', because repentence is a sign of grace.

A lighter superstition about the plant is that it will thrive better in the garden if it is stolen, rather than bought or exchanged. The variety which is illustrated is the one most generally grown now, and this forms a solid dome of blue-green that is a pleasing contrast to all the other greens of the garden. Rue grows best in semi-shade.

1

3

2

Now will he sit under a medlar-tree,
And wish his mistress were that kind of fruit
As maids call medlars when they laugh alone.
                    Mercutio – *Romeo and Juliet*, II. i. 34

. . . and thy broom-groves,
Whose shadow the dismissed bachelor loves,
Being lass-lorn:
                    Iris – *The Tempest*, IV. i. 66

1 MEDLAR
Mespilus germanica

The Medlar in maturity grows more often into a huge spreading bush which is as broad as it is high, with leafy skirts frequently trailing down to touch the ground. The Medlar fruits, which look like enlarged brown hips with the seeds exposed to view, are generally eaten when they are soft, or 'bletted' which means that the Medlars should be ripe almost to the point of rottenness. Medlars were often used as a simile for loose women in Shakespeare's day, and he uses this again in *Measure for Measure* where Lucio is telling the truth about his amours: '. . . but I was fain to forswear it: they would else have married me to the rotten medlar' (IV. iii. 183).

2 BROOM
Cytisus scoparius

The Broom was formerly called *Planta genista*, and as such it gave its name to the Royal line of the Plantagenets.

A hillside covered with wild Broom in flower is a lovely sight in May, and there are many garden varieties with flowers of solid colour or various combinations of white, cream, yellow, pink, red or crimson.

Cultivated varieties of Broom have only a short life-span – about ten years is the maximum. After this, the evergreen branches will begin to die, giving the shrub a very untidy and neglected appearance. There is no possibility of any remedial treatment: the bush is dying and should be pulled out, the soil that it grew in replaced with some from another part of the garden and a replacement can then be planted.

Like to a vagabond flag upon the stream,
Goes to and back, lackeying the varying tide,
Octavius Caesar – *Antony and Cleopatra*, I. iv. 45

A wreath of bullrush rounded;
Wooer – *The Two Noble Kinsmen*, IV. i. 84

. . . thick set with reeds and sedges,
Wooer – *The Two Noble Kinsmen*, IV. i. 54

More rushes, more rushes.
First Groom – *2 Henry* IV, V. v. 1

1 FLAG
Iris pseudacorus

In England, wild Irises are often called 'Flags'; although this word has been used as a general title for almost any sword-leaved waterside plant since Biblical times.

2 BULRUSH
Typha latifolia

The true Bulrush (*Scirpus lacustris*) is another waterside plant that bears no resemblance to the traditional 'Bulrush' of the painting, which is botanically a Reedmace. The cylindrical seed-heads are at first green and later turn to the familiar rich velvety-brown of the picture books.

3 REED
Phragmites australis

The word 'Reed' is loosely used for any grassy-leaved waterside plant, and in literature the growing plant has often symbolised weakness, submission and humility.

4 SEDGE
Carex sylvatica

Similarly, the word 'sedge' has come to mean almost any grassy plant that grows in damp places.

5 RUSH
(Woodrush)
Luzula sylvatica

Rushes of several kinds were used in medieval times as replaceable floor-coverings for mansions and churches.

Rush-rings were originally plaited for honest country betrothals, but this custom fell into disuse because of the 'mock-marriages' so easily practised.

1

5

3

2

4

. . . I have sent him, where a cedar,
Higher than all the rest, spreads like a plane,
Fast by a brook;
Jailer's Daughter – *The Two Noble Kinsmen*, II. vi. 4

There is a willow grows aslant a brook,
That shows his hoar leaves in the glassy stream;
Gertrude – *Hamlet*, IV. vii. 167

1 CEDAR
(Cedar of Lebanon)
Cedrus libani

The characteristic silhouette of the Cedar of Lebenon would not have been seen in the British Isles until early in 1700, because the earliest recorded planting of this majestic tree was not until 1676. Shakespeare would only have known of the Cedar from the many Biblical mentions of it, where it is always described as being the most kingly of trees.

2 PLANE
(London Plane)
Platanus x acerifolia

The London Plane is a beautiful tree of streets and city parks, but it is not native to the British Isles or even to Europe. It was admired by Greeks and Romans alike, who introduced it from the East and planted it extensively. The Plane tree grows surprisingly well in areas of traffic pollution and restricted root-room and this is why it is still being planted, centuries later.

3 WILLOW
(White Willow)
Salix alba

The Willow seems always to have been associated with sadness, mourning and weeping, as may be realised by the many folk songs and early poems that name this unhappy tree. The White Willow of the illustration is the tree that Shakespeare would have known, because it is native to the British Isles, whereas the Weeping Willow *Salix babylonica* (which by its drooping habit is far more indicative of woe) is a much later introduction.

It is said that the first Weeping Willow grew from a twig untwisted from a basket of figs that had been sent from Turkey; this twig was planted and grew into the familiar and ornamental waterside tree.

1

3

2

And here I prophesy: this brawl to-day,
Grown to this faction in the Temple-garden,
Shall send between the red rose and the white
A thousand souls to death and deadly night.
                    Earl of Warwick – *1 Henry VI*, II. iv. 124

The roses fearfully on thorns did stand,
One blushing shame, another white despair;
A third, nor red nor white, had stol'n of both,
And to his robbery had annex'd thy breath;
                    Sonnet XCIX

1 'APOTHECARY'S ROSE'
Rosa officinalis

The 'Apothecary's Rose', *Rosa officinalis*, was brought to the British Isles from France for medicinal purposes, and remained unchanged in character and appearance since those early days; it is considered by many to be the Red Rose of Lancaster.

2 'JACOBITE ROSE'
Rosa x alba maxima

The 'Jacobite Rose', *Rosa x alba maxima*, is a very ancient rose, and may well have been known by Shakespeare before it became the emblem of Bonnie Prince Charlie's supporters during the Jacobite rebellion some seventy years later. The perfumed tangle of rose history can never be fully unravelled, and it is really a matter of conjecture as to whether this was the white rose chosen to be the emblem of the Yorkists.

3 'ROSA MUNDI'
Rosa gallica versicolor
4 'YORK AND LANCASTER'
Rosa damascena versicolor

The variegated Gallica rose called 'Rosa Mundi' is known to have been in cultivation for over 500 years, and its white petals are always streaked and splashed with deep carmine; when examined closely, the white petals are seen to be the palest of pale pink, and no two flowers on the same bush are ever alike in colour. 'Rosa Mundi' is said to have been named after Fair Rosamond, mistress of King Henry II who lived in the twelfth century. Because of this rose's very definite pied colouration, this may well have been the one in Shakespeare's mind when he wrote the lines in Sonnet XCIX. The alternative Damask rose 'York and Lancaster' has only been known since 1629, and Shakespeare would therefore never have seen it; much subsequent legend has grown up around this rose because in a good plant the petals of the flower are intermingled pink and white.

Sleep thou, and I will wind thee in my arms.
Fairies, be gone, and be all ways away.
So doth the woodbine the sweet honeysuckle
Gently entwist; the female ivy so
Enrings the barky fingers of the elm.
Titania – *A Midsummer-Night's Dream*, IV. i. 45

Bind fast his corky arms.
Cornwall – *King Lear*, III. vii. 28

1 WOODBINE,
HONEYSUCKLE
Lonicera periclymenum

During Shakespeare's time these two names were given to the same climbing plant (see page 72) but before this period the name 'Woodbine' was loosely applied to almost any climbing growth, and 'Honeysuckle' could have meant any sweet-scented flower, even a Primrose.

2 IVY
Hedera helix

For many years the Ivy was considered to be a parasite, living off its host-tree by means of the small adventitious rootlets that are to be found throughout the length of the climbing stem. It is known today that these small but powerful aerial roots merely serve to attach the Ivy firmly to wall or tree-trunk.

3 ELM
Ulmus procera

The landscape of Britain has been changed for ever by the ravages of a small beetle, the carrier of the fungus of Dutch Elm disease that killed this noble tree, once a loved and familiar part of almost every country scene in the British Isles.

4 CORK
Quercus suber

The Cork Oak was not introduced into the British Isles until quite late in the seventeenth century, and Shakespeare would never have seen the actual tree, though he would have been very familiar with the use of corks as stoppers for wine-flagons and as bungs for wine-casks. The main use for the bark of the tree in those days was in shoemaking.

> *. . . and nothing teems*
> *But hateful docks, rough thistles, kecksies, burs,*
> *Losing both beauty and utility.*
> Duke of Burgundy – *Henry V*, V. ii. 51

1 DOCK
Rumex conglomeratus

Docks are synonymous with dereliction and neglect, because no farmer will permit them to spread over good grazing land. Cattle and horses eat all round them, so the docks will multiply unhindered.

It is a curious fact that wherever stinging nettles are found a dock plant will not be far away, its cool leaves so soothing to the pain of nettle-stings.

2 THISTLE
Onopordum acanthium

Thistles are equally synonymous with neglect, but not necessarily with poor soil; like many other weeds, they will grow even larger and finer on good ground. The Thistle of the illustration is the handsomest of the British species, and a well-grown specimen standing alone looks like an enormous silvery candelabrum.

Onopordum is reputed to be the thistle that saved Scotland, and the story goes that the Scots were camped at night, exhausted from battle with marauding Danish raiders. The raiders had followed the Scots and were stealthily attempting to surround the camp in order to slaughter their enemies, and in order to achieve complete silence the Danes crept barefoot. They might have succeeded in their purpose, had not one of their number inadvertently trodden on a thistle in the darkness. His howl of pain aroused the camp and the Scots were able to defend themselves and their kingdom.

3 KECKSIE
(Hogweed)
Heracleum sphondyllium

Kecksies are the dried stems of almost any of the umbellifer family, but more particularly of the Hogweed, so named because it was and still is an excellent pig-food.

4 BUR
Arctium lappa

Nature has evolved an excellent method of seed-dispersal for this plant – the hooked seeds transfer themselves lightly and easily to the coat of passing beast or man and so are inevitably carried a considerable distance from the parent plant.

The root can be used medicinally to alleviate rheumatic pain, and the giant leaves make a good poultice for bruises.

> . . . why, he was met even now
> As mad as the vex'd sea; singing aloud;
> Crown'd with rank fumiter and furrow-weeds,
> With bur-docks, hemlock, nettles, cuckoo-flowers,
> Darnel, . . .
> Cordelia – *King Lear*, IV. iv. 1

1 FUMITER
(Fumitory)
Fumaria officinalis

The delicate-looking Fumitory (now mostly found on forgotten allotments) was formerly a serious weed of agriculture, being quite capable of smothering whole fields of corn.

2 FURROW-WEEDS

These would have been any ploughland weeds which would have grown as sturdily then as they do now. Modern farming methods mean that English cornfields are, alas, no longer jewelled with sapphire Cornflowers and garnet Poppies. The illustration shows the latter.

3 CUCKOO-FLOWER
Ranunculus repens

Regional names for wild flowers varied greatly and 'Cuckoo-flowers' might have been almost any spring flower such as the Wood-Anemone, Red Campion, Ragged Robin, Bluebell, Wood-Sorrel or the Early Purple Orchid. It is now generally assumed that the Cuckoo-flowers are here meant to be Buttercups, though this name was not in general use until the middle of the eighteenth century.

4 DARNEL
Lolium temulentum

Darnel was known as a noxious weed of the cornfield ever since Biblical times, because the presence of the black seeds made visible specks in the flour, greatly depreciating the value of the crop. Darnel is not now known in England, however, except as a very scarce introduction.

5 BURDOCK
Arctium pubens

The Burdock is a large and handsome plant when seen growing naturally by the waterside, but it is here classed as an unwanted weed. The burs hook themselves on to passing animals (and humans) and the seeds are thus dispersed over enormous distances.

6 HEMLOCK
Conium maculatum

Four hundred years before the life of Christ, the philosopher Socrates took his last drink, always supposed to have been a distillation of Hemlock. With its musty smell and purple-spotted stems, the plant looks and smells as sinister as its reputation.

7 NETTLE
Urtica dioica

Nettles are so well known as to need no description, and as Culpepper said 'they may be found by feeling in the darkest night'.

[66]

What's in a name? that which we call a rose
By any other name would smell as sweet;
> Juliet − *Romeo and Juliet*, II. ii. 43

1 'DAINTY MAID'
Floribunda

2 'DR W. VAN
FLEET'
Climbing Rose

3 Species Rose
Rosa willmottiae

These simple words about a rose must surely be the best-known and most often quoted throughout the world. So it is with roses − best known of all flowers, and portrayed in various styles and degrees of accuracy from the earliest of civilisations until the present day. There are roses of many colours (except the elusive blue) and all heights and habits, from the miniatures with their perfect and doll-size flowers, the gigantic Himalayan ramblers that can entirely cover an old apple tree with a cascading foam of flowers, the pale and charming 'muddled' blooms of the historic old roses, to the perfectly sculptured shapes of the roses of today.

All roses have their roots as firmly in history as in the prepared soil of palace or pavilion, public park or private home. The newest rose at this year's show may have taken ten years (or more) of careful selection, as might each of its parents, and it is likely that one of the grandparents might have been a strong-growing wild rose unchanged since its discovery by the plant-hunters of a hundred years ago.

The illustration shows three pink roses of widely differing types: 'Dainty Maid' is a striking single rose, bred in Norfolk in 1938, whose name and appearance evokes the dew-fresh pink and white complexion of a young girl of long ago. 'Dr W. van Fleet' is an old favourite of 1910, flowering abundantly in early summer; its parentage is recorded as being R. *wichuraiana* x 'Sofrano' x 'Souvenir du President Carnot'. *Rosa wichuraiana* came from the far East in about 1880 and has been used by rose-breeders ever since.

The third rose is R. *willmottiae*, discovered on the Chinese-Tibetan border in 1904 by E. H. Wilson and named after that famous English gardener, Miss Ellen Willmott. This is a 'wild' rose, whose ferny foliage is starred for only one month in the year with flat lilac-pink flowers that open thickly all along the arching stems.

1

2

3

And let the stinking elder, grief, untwine
His perishing root with the increasing vine!
Arviragus – *Cymbeline*, IV. ii. 59

1 ELDER
Sambucus nigra

There was a time when nothing good was ever said of an Elder-tree; it was evil-smelling, it was unlucky to burn as firewood, it must not be used in boat building or to make household furniture, and Judas Iscariot was reputed to have hung himself from its branches. Even the whips of the drivers of horse-drawn hearses were once especially made of Elder-wood, which was considered to be protection against the new spirits of the newly-dead.

All this dark and gloomy superstition was balanced by the simultaneous belief in the efficacy of the tree's powers to drive away evil spirits, because the elder-tree belonged to Hulda, the Scandinavian goddess of Love. It was believed that if an Elder tree grew in a garden, the owner would die peacefully in his bed. Wind instruments (flutes, pipes, and whistles) were made from the wood, although the tree's Latin name *Sambuca* means a stringed instrument. More particularly on the credit side are the wines that can be made from fruit and flowers – the delicate Elderflower of late spring and the more robust and ruby-glowing Elderberry wine of autumn. Elderflowers are still used to make lotions and creams; a soothing ointment for chilblains can be made from the leaves; and the flowers make a remedial tea or tisane for colds and chills. An Elder tree is sombre when not in flower, and nothing else will grow in the shadow of its branches.

2 VINE
Vitis vinifera

The vine has been a solace to man since earliest civilisation, and very many books have been written in very many languages about viticulture. Yet another proof that our British summers were warmer in former years is found in ancient records of the many large vineyards that were known to exist, and the Domesday Book lists thirty-eight of these. It is interesting to note that several thriving industries connected with the growing and harvesting of particular plants not native to these islands were very successful for many years and were then quite suddenly discontinued. Examples of this are Lavender, Flax, Saffron, Hemp, Liquorice (still being grown in a small way at Pontefract) and, of course, the Vine.

I

2

I know a bank where the wild thyme blows,
Where oxlips and the nodding violet grows;
Quite over-canopied with luscious woodbine,
With sweet musk-roses, and with eglantine:
Oberon – *A Midsummer Night's Dream*, II. i. 249

1 THYME
Thymus drucei

This is one of the most famous quotations of all from the works of Shakespeare, and certainly one of the most evocative of the English countryside. Wild Thyme grows on chalky hillsides, and its mounds of rose-coloured blooms are often seen growing on disused ant-hills, which provide the finest textured of all growing mediums.

2 OXLIP
Primula elatior

When Shakespeare spoke of groups of flowers, he almost always placed them in their seasons of flowering, except in this particular case. Oxlips flower in the spring, side by side with their cousins the Primrose and the Cowslip, and are long over by the time all the other flowers of the quotation come into bloom. However, the leaves are almost evergreen, and can be easily seen among the later-flowering 'nodding violets'.

3 VIOLET
Viola canina

The short-stalked and scentless Dog Violet grows on sunny banks and hillsides, where its clear blue-mauve flowers seem to jewel the turf, kept short by sheep and rabbits.

4 WOODBINE
(Honeysuckle)
Lonicera periclymenum

There is still argument about Shakespeare's use of both names for the Honeysuckle, but it is suggested that the name 'Woodbine' was applied in a general way to the plant, and 'Honeysuckle' more specifically to the flowers.

This sweet-scented climbing flower of hedge and woodside is more powerful than it looks, because the trunk of the host-tree is often spirally scored by the ever-growing and ever-thickening stem of the honeysuckle.

5 MUSK-ROSE
Rosa arvensis

Rose history is as tangled as Titania's bower, but most of the historians agree that by 'musk-rose' Shakespeare meant our native white *Rosa arvensis*, which climbs the hedgerow trees and festoons them with dark-stemmed hanging garlands of starry single flowers, more noticeably scented in damp weather.

6 EGLANTINE
(Sweetbriar)
Rosa rubiginosa

This wild rose can perfume the air for yards around, especially when the weather conditions alternate with sunshine and showers. It is the leaves that give off the delicious apple scent, more fragrant than the foliage of any other rose.

4

2

5

6

I

3

I have seen roses damask'd, red and white,
But no such roses see I in her cheeks;
Sonnet CXXX

. . . with two Provincial roses on my razed shoes,
Hamlet – *Hamlet*, III. ii. 288

DAMASK ROSES
('Madame Hardy' 1 and
'Ispahan' 2)

CENTIFOLIA ROSE
('Tour de Malakoff' 3)

CENTIFOLIA MOSS
('William Lobb' 4)

Of the four roses illustrated opposite, the damask 'Madame Hardy' has the most ancient lineage, being named after the wife of the director of the Luxembourg gardens in 1832. 'Madame Hardy' is a cross between *Rosa damascena* and *Rosa centifolia* and therefore inherits the exquisite scent and the many petals of its parents.

'Ispahan' has a longer flowering season than the other damasks and it has the loosely recurving outer petals that are very characteristic of these roses. This is one of the many roses that are grown in Bulgaria for the famous attar.

The 'Provincial Roses' of the quotation are Centifolia roses from Provence, in France, and should not be confused with the Provins rose (which is a Gallica) and which is also from France. Fashionable gallants of the times often had their elegant 'razed' (ie slashed) shoes adorned with artificial flowers which were sometimes embroidered as well; roses and pinks were the favourites (see quotation on page 78).

The Centifolia rose was developed in Holland from the end of the sixteenth century onwards, and these roses often featured in the magnificent flower-pieces of the Dutch old masters.

'Tour de Malakoff' is a vigorous old Centifolia of 1856, with long shoots bearing large blooms that droop on slender flower-stems. The centre petals are often bright cerise at first, but as the flower ages most of the petals change to a delicate, veined lavender-grey, though some of the bright cerise petals still retain their colour.

'William Lobb' is a very tall and strong-growing moss-rose which needs to be planted against a solid support. The flowers open as a rich rose-purple which gradually fades to mauve, and the flower cluster may be in several stages and shades of development, which contrasts well with the rich green 'moss' of the calyxes.

MADONNA LILY
Lilium candidum

The white satin petals of the Madonna Lily have always been a symbol of immaculate purity. The flower has accordingly become associated with legends of the Virgin Mary, after whom it is named.

Lilies of all kinds have been cultivated for thousands of years, and the Madonna Lily is one of the oldest species known to gardeners; pictures of it are clearly recognisable on the frescoes and vases of ancient Egypt and Crete.

This particular lily was once so easily grown that it was a normal plant of many a cottage garden; it seemed to need no special treatment or cossetting, and would come up year after year, the clumps increasing in size and scented beauty. Nowadays, however, this is a lily that is regarded as something of a pariah by gardeners with a collection of species lilies, because *Lilium candidum* harbours viral diseases such as Echinocystis and Speciosum Fleck; these will infect not only other lilies but also grain and vegetables.

If this variety is grown, it does well in pots, which can be moved into position just as the flowers are about to open. The scent of a clump of these lilies on a warm, still summer evening is one of a gardener's great rewards. The bulbs should be planted on a bed of silver-sand for good drainage and to discourage the small black slugs that do so much subterranean damage. These lilies are the only variety that should be planted with the tip of the bulb covered only lightly with soil, and the bulbs should be moved and planted only in late summer, after they have flowered and become dormant.

The flower-stems can reach a height of six feet when grown under favourable conditions, which are a free-draining alkaline soil, a cool root situation, plenty of moisture during the growing season, and sun to grow to. The bulbs resent disturbance once established.

Romeo: *Pink for flower.*
Mercutio: *Right.*
Romeo: *Why, then is my pump well flowered.*
                    Romeo and Juliet, II. iv. 62

for though the camomile, the more it is trodden
on the faster it grows, yet youth, the more it is
wasted the sooner it wears.
                    Falstaff – *1 Henry IV*, II. iv. 441

he capers, he dances, he has eyes of youth, he
writes verses, he speaks holiday . . .
he will carry't, he will carry't; 'tis in his buttons; he will carry't.
                    Host – *The Merry Wives of Windsor*, III, ii. 67

1 PINK
Dianthus allwoodii

'Pinksten' was the German word for Pentecost (the seventh Sunday after Easter) and 'Pinkstens' were therefore flowers that bloomed only at Pentecost; it was some time before the name 'Pink' was applied to these members of the *Dianthus* family, and the colour-name was taken from the plant, not the other way about, as may be thought, 'Pinckes' were much esteemed in Tudor gardens. For the significance of the quotation, see page 74.

2 CAMOMILE
(Chamomile)
Anthemis nobilis

Chamomile plants thrive on being trodden upon (though not too heavily), and make a wonderfully aromatic path. Chamomile tea was an old-fashioned remedy for hysteria in women, with a safely soothing and calming effect. The plant was used by all the old herbalists for a variety of ailments. A modern use for Chamomile is as an excellent shampoo to lighten naturally fair hair.

3 BATCHELOR'S
BUTTONS
Ranunculus acris flore pleno

In the Middle Ages small flowers were carried in a man's pocket or under a girl's apron as a guide to success in love. If they remained fresh, the owner would gain his heart's desire; if they withered, all would be lost. ''Tis in his buttons' therefore came to mean 'he will be successful'.

The name 'Batchelor's Buttons' has been loosely applied to several small many-petalled cottage-garden flowers, among them the Double Buttercup *Ranunculus acris flora plena*. The name is the cause of much inconclusive argument among gardeners.

Lark's-heels trim;
Introductory Song – *The Two Noble Kinsmen*

And beauty that the tyrant oft reclaims
Shall to my flaming wrath be oil and flax.
Young Clifford – *2 Henry VI*, V. ii. 54

1 LARKS-HEEL
(Larkspur)
Delphinium orientale

The annual Larkspur of cottage gardens is a native of North Africa and central and southern Europe. The flowers come in every shade of blue, mauve and pink, and there is a white variety. The old herbalists used the plant medicinally, and it was known by several similar names: 'Lark's-toes', 'Lark's-claws' and, nowadays, 'Larkspur'. The perennial Larkspur is the well known Delphinium (*D. grandiflorum*) which was introduced into England early in the eighteenth century. Gerard knew the annual variety well.

2 LARKS-HEEL
(Nasturtium)
Tropaeolum majus

The flower that is now known as 'Nasturtium' was called 'Yellow Lark's-Heels' by the Elizabethans. They had several names for it as it was then a very new introduction from the West Indies. The Spanish explorers brought seeds of different varieties back to Spain, whence the flower was gradually introduced into the gardens of Europe. The yellow variety was the one most commonly grown, and that great gardener, Parkinson, prized it highly, calling it 'Nasturtium Indicum' or 'Nastnerzo de las Indias' because the word 'Indies' became the general name of all the Spanish colonies in Central and Southern America.

3 FLAX
Linum narbonnense

The Flax plant has been associated with the manufacture of linen and medicines since remote history. It is a delicate little plant with wiry, fine-leaved stems and flowers of an exquisite pure blue. Linseed oil is made from the seeds of *Linum usitatissimum* (this variety has smaller, paler flowers) which is the species grown commercially for the production of the oil used in the manufacture of paints, varnishes and polishes; the residual matter is made into cattle-cake. The oil is highly inflammable. The stem-fibre when processed is made into linen, which has an exceedingly long life; linen-wrapped mummies have been accurately dated at over 4,000 years old.

LILY

vars. *1 Lilium pyrenaicum*
2 Lilium martagon
3 Lilium
'Harlequin' hybrid

The lily family is a very large one, and many of its members still grow in the wild places of the earth. In addition to the true lilies there are other bulbous subjects such as Fritillaries, Tulips, Scillas, Hyacinths and Bluebells (Endymion) while those with rhizomatious roots are Hostas, Agapanthus and the Aloe; all are of the family Liliaceae.

Lily bulbs are made up of a number of adhering 'scales' and have no protective skin; they are therefore very easily damaged. They should never be allowed to dry out, and incorrect storage of the lifted bulbs is often the cause of expensive failure in lily culture.

Lilies do not like being baked in the sun; neither do they like a boggy or wet position. All varieties need good drainage and most, though not all, dislike lime in the soil.

There are lilies of all heights and sizes, and all colours except blue. The tiny variety 'Tom Thumb' is only 16 inches high and needs to be grown under glass, whereas the tall and majestic *Cardiocrinum giganteum* from the Himalayas (now included in the genus *Lilium*) can grow to a towering 12 feet in ideal open woodland conditions.

Lily flowers may be trumpet-shaped, like the old favourite, *Lilium regale*, which is pink and white, heavily scented and easy to grow; bowl-shaped, like the many new and beautiful Oriental hybrids, or the petals may be tightly recurved like a Turk's cap; the illustration shows two varieties of these Turk's Cap lilies, *Lilium pyrenaicum* and *Lilium martagon*, both of which are European wild flowers. Some lilies may be few-flowered, whereas others like *Lilium auratum*, the 'Golden-rayed Lily of Japan', may have as many as twenty or thirty huge white and gold flowers at the top of a six-foot stem. Lilies like this which need support in bad weather should be strongly but inconspicuously staked, whereas the spidery lightness of a many-flowered modern Martagon hybrid needs no such attention.

what sayest thou, my fair flower-de-luce?
King Henry – *Henry V*, V. ii. 224

Iris   *Dramatis persona, The Tempest*

1 FLOWER-DE-
LUCE
(Bearded Iris)
Iris germanica

There has always been controversy as to which flower Shakespeare
knew as the 'flower-de-luce'. One legend is as follows. In the sixth
century, King Clovis (the Frankish King) was about to fight a
battle; before he fought, he prayed for victory to his wife's Christian
God. The king won the day, and in gratitude became converted to
Christianity, and thereafter changed the emblems on his banner from
three toads to three Irises, the flowers of the Virgin Mary. Hundreds
of years later, King Louis VII of France used the same emblems
when setting forth on his crusade to the Holy Land. The Iris then
became known as the *Fleur de Louis*. Another story is that a
vanquished French king was fleeing for his life from a battlefield,
closely pursued by his victors. Coming upon the river Lys (on the
borders of Flanders) he saw the Irises all in bloom and, knowing
that these flowers grew only in shallow water, he spurred his horse
across what proved to be a ford, unseen by his foes. Grateful for his
merciful deliverance, he adopted the stylised Iris as his heraldic
symbol, and it then became known as the *Fleur de Lys*, which became
the symbolic flower of France as the Rose is of England. The Iris has
always been portrayed as a royal flower by the great painters of the
Renaissance and earlier, and stylised versions of it have appeared on
the armorial bearings of kings and emperors; the flower itself is said
to be the origin of the sceptre, the three petals representing faith,
valour and wisdom.

2 IRIS
(Englsih Iris)
Iris xiphioides

Some of the flowers which Shakespeare called 'lilies' have today
been reclassified by the botanists into the family *Iridaceae*. This is
illustrated in the quotation from *The Winter's Tale* (IV. iv. 126),
'lilies of all kinds, the flower-de-luce being one'. The various
spellings *fleur-de-lys, fleur de lis*, or Shakespeare's own 'flower-de-luce'
are all assumed to mean the same flower, the Iris, named after the
goddess Iris because of the rich variety of the rainbow-hued
blossoms. There are now many kinds and colours of garden Irises
which have been collected from all over the world.

I

2

. . . all prisoners, sir,
In the line-grove which weather-fends your cell;
Ariel – *The Tempest*, V. i. 9

LINE
(Lime)
Tilia x europaea

The name 'Lime' for the Line or Linden is a comparatively modern term.

A Lime tree that has grown to full maturity is one of the tallest and most beautiful trees of the English countryside now that the Elm is no more, and when a large Lime tree is in full bloom the scent will perfume the whole neighbourhood, particularly in still weather.

The Lime was formerly much planted as an avenue tree or in public parks and gardens, but it has lost favour with civic gardeners for the following reasons: it comes late into leaf in spring, and sheds its leaves very early in autumn; it is much afflicted by Honeydew (a secretion of Aphids); it grows very large and the branches have to be pruned or pollarded; and it produces sheaves of suckers at the base of the tree-bole. Nevertheless a Lime tree in blossom seems to breathe forth the essence of an English summer, and when the flowers are gathered and made into sweet-scented pillows and sachets they evoke instant memories of warm June days, even in the darkest and coldest of the winter months. *Tilleul*, or Lime-flower tea, is a favourite beverage in France. The wood of the tree was formerly much in demand by wood-carvers, because it is white and close-grained and is never attacked by woodworm. The most famous wood-carver of them all, Grinling Gibbons, used Lime-wood for his incredibly delicate carvings of fruit, flowers, lace and musical instruments, which are as perfect now as when they were first carved. In the USA the tree is known as Basswood, and is still much used for beehive frames because the wood is quite free from taint of any kind.

[86]

> *the fairest flowers o' the season*
> *Are our carnations and streak'd gillyvors,*
> Perdita – *The Winter's Tale*, IV. iv. 81

> *Their sweetest shade a grove of cypress trees!*
> Duke of Suffolk – *2 Henry VI*, III. ii. 323

1 CARNATION, GILLYVOR
Dianthus caryophyllus

The carnation has from earliest times been grown and used as a formal flower for celebrations, and the name 'Carnation' comes from the word 'coronation' which in turn is derived from the Latin *Corona*, 'crown'. The names Gilloflower, Gillyflower and Gilofre are all easily traceable to *caryophyllus* which means 'nut-leaved'. Inappropriate though this name is for the silver-grey leaves of the Carnation, it was nevertheless bestowed on it because the flowers were scented like the Clove tree (which was then *Eugenia caryophyllata*).

In medieval times there were hundreds of varieties of Carnations now forever lost to us; they were different in shape and some of the charming and evocative names of yesterday were the Orange Tawny Gillyflower, the Gray Hulo, the Red Hulo, the Blue Hulo and the Striped Savage. Parkinson separated the Gillyflowers from the Carnations in his lists, and among his favourites were The Lustie Gallant, Ruffling Robin, the Pale Pageant, the Sad Pageant, Master Bradshawe his Dainty Lady, and Master Tuggie his Princess.

2 CYPRESS
(Funeral Cypress)
Cupressus sempervirens

There is a legend about the dark and pencil-thin Cypress of the Mediterranean shores that warns the traveller never to fall asleep in its shade, because the evil roots, greedy for intelligence, will grow into the sleeper's brain, to steal away his mind and he will wake up mad.

> *Of all flowers,*
> *Methinks a rose is best.*
> Emilia – *The Two Noble Kinsmen*, II. ii. 135

ROSE var. 'Guinee'

The roses that Shakespeare would have known (there are over a hundred references to roses in his writings) were very different from those that are grown today. A few of the old roses have survived and are still being grown, and it is almost certain that the varieties 'Great Maiden's Blush', *Rosa gallica versicolor* 'Rosa Mundi', and *Rosa officinalis* 'The Apothecary's Rose' are the same today as they were some four hundred years ago. The red roses that Shakespeare knew were unlikely to be as richly-coloured as the illustration, which is a modern climbing rose (1938). Most of the old 'red' roses were various shades of deep pink or cerise. Shakespeare's white rose is thought to be *Rosa x alba maxima*, later to become the 'Jacobite Rose' (see page 60).

The 'Provincial rose' mentioned by Shakespeare is probably the old Provencal rose, once called 'Hundred-leaved rose'. A typical example still being grown is 'Rose de Meaux' which was named after a Bishop who loved all flowers, particularly roses. The 'Rose of May' that Ophelia was compared to by Laertes was almost certainly the old early-flowering Cinnamon rose beloved by the Victorians.

The musk-scented roses of our time may be climbers with that giant of scent and size, *Rosa moschata*, in their pedigree, or they may be richly scented bushes of varying heights and habits. Shakespeare's original musk roses would have been lost to cultivation long years ago, but their places are taken today by a beautiful army of hybrid musk roses such as 'Daybreak', 'Moonlight', 'Penelope', 'Pax', 'Thisbe' and many others. It is known that musk-scented flowers smelt a great deal stronger in former times; the curious and unexplained phenomenon of the musk-flower, *Mimulus moschatus*, losing its scent simultaneously all over the world in 1914 is indicative of this.

Damask roses originated in the East, and have been grown for their scent for thousands of years. Attar of roses was once so highly valued that a phial of the rich perfume was worth more than its own weight in gold.

The Sweetbriar or Eglantine is the only native rose named by Shakespeare and it is illustrated on p. 73.

Not poppy, nor mandragora,
Nor all the drowsy syrups of the world,
Shall ever medicine thee to that sweet sleep
Which thou owedst yesterday.
Iago – Othello, III. iii. 330

Under the cool shade of a sycamore
I thought to close mine eyes some half an hour;
Boyet – *Love's Labour's Lost*, V. ii. 89

1 POPPY
Papaver somniferum

The poppy of the quotation was certainly the Opium poppy, which has been used as an anaesthetic as well as a narcotic since earliest times. The true Opium poppy is not cultivated in Northern Europe for medicinal purposes because the climate is not warm enough, though as a garden annual it spreads very freely, and occurs in a single or very double form in many shades, from silvery white with a violet-black blotch to pale lilac, pink, mauve, cerise or crimson. The true Opium poppy is the plant that produces morphine and its derivative, the narcotic hallucinatory drug, heroin.

2 MANDRAGORA
(Mandrake)
Mandragora officinarum

The Mandrake was used a great deal in medieval times and before as an aid to fecundity in women. This use for the plant would seem to date from the story of Rachel and Leah in Genesis XXX: 14–17. At what period *fear* of the plant became widespread is not known, but it may have been a practical way of ensuring the continuation of a valuable plant that was not common in any case, and which took many years to grow to the required size and traditional man-shape (it has protrusions which resemble arms and legs). It was said that the Mandrake screamed as it was drawn out of the earth, and that the sound of this scream presaged certain death to any who heard it. In order, therefore, to stay alive and continue the very lucrative occupation of Mandrake-growing and selling, the diggers used a black dog to haul the root from the soil, and themselves stopped up their ears. The illustration is of *Mandragora vernalis* which is native to Northern Italy and Western Yugoslavia.

3 SYCAMORE
Acer pseudoplatanus

The Sycamore of the Bible is the Zicamine or Fig-Mulberry *Ficus sycomorus* which is native to the Middle East and which is grown for its fruit and as a shade-tree. The Sycamore of the British Isles is no relation to this tree at all, but because it also produces a solid shadow the early writers applied the name Sycamore to almost any substantial shade-tree. Sycamores are quick-growing and were formerly planted near man's habitation for a variety of uses. Least pleasant of these was as a gallows-tree, and the Sycamore was therefore called a 'dool' or grief tree, particularly in Scotland.

That the united vessel of their blood,
Mingled with venom of suggestion —
As, force perforce, the age will pour it in —
Shall never leak, though it do work as strong
As aconitum or rash gunpowder.
　　　　　King Henry – *2 Henry IV*, IV. iv. 44

. . . thou hemp-seed!
　　　　　Mistress Quickly – *2 Henry IV*, II. i. 64

1 ACONITUM, ACONITE, MONK'S HOOD
Aconitum napellus

Aconite or Monk's Hood was introduced into England many hundreds of years ago as a medicinal plant, and mention of it and its fatal properties are to be found in tenth-century manuscripts. All parts of the plant, even the pollen-dust, are extremely poisonous and its other old name of 'Wolf's Bane' was derived from its use in Europe for destroying wolves. In medieval time poison was used very much more often than it is today, and every man grew his own – more to dispose of vermin than of his neighbour. Aconite is still used today as a sedative and as an anodyne, and can still sometimes be found in very old cottage gardens where its stately spires of blue flowers can be seen in early summer, rather resembling Delphiniums, to which Aconite is closely related.

2 HEMP
Cannabis sativa

Shakespeare used the word 'Hemp' in its connotation with rope in several references, but not the one above. The plant was an introduction to England for the purposes of rope, cordage and canvas making, and was extensively grown, because England was fast becoming an important maritime nation. Hemp came originally from India, but seemed to thrive in almost any climate then as it still does today. The plant is a tall-growing spiky-leaved annual that is of great use medicinally as a pain-killer, but it is as the hallucinatory drug Marijuana, Cannabis, Indian Hemp or Hashish that it is best known today. When smoked, Indian Hemp produces an exhilarating intoxication which acts on the higher nerve-centres, though its effect depends on the temperament of the individual concerned. Regrettably the drug needs to be taken in ascending quantities to produce the same effect. The Hemp plant is still grown for its fibre in natural rope-making.

The food that to him now is as luscious as
locusts, shall be to him shortly as bitter as
coloquintida.
Iago – *Othello*, I. iii. 354

Thy sugar'd tongue to bitter wormwood taste:
The Rape of Lucrece 893

And sweetens, in the suff'ring pangs it bears,
The aloes of all forces, shocks, and fears.
A Lover's Complaint 273

LOCUST
(1, fruit, and 1a, leaves)
Ceratonia siliqua

The Locust of the quotation is the fruit of the Carob tree. In Biblical times it was used as animal fodder, but today Carob fruit is recognised as being an important constituent in natural foods. The actual trees were sometimes grown in Britain as curiosities by herbalists both before and during Shakespeare's lifetime. It is recorded that they never bore flowers or fruit.

2 COLOQUINTIDA
Citrullus colocynthus

This plant has been grown for medicinal purposes since earliest times, and was known as the 'Bitter Apple' from its exceedingly bitter and nauseous taste. It was imported into Britain from Turkey long before the sixteenth century, and sometimes grown as a curiosity in the collections of the herbalists. It is poisonous even in very small quantities, and was always used in conjunction with other drug plants.

3 WORMWOOD
Artemisia absinthium

Wormwood is almost a synonym for bitterness of taste, but to the ancient Greeks it was a most beneficial herb, and was used with skill to alleviate many illnesses. It is a prime ingredient of the liqueur Absinthe, prolonged addiction to which causes mental disturbance and even madness.

4 ALOE
Aloe thomsoniae

The Aloe is another synonym for bitterness, but it was formerly associated with the costly spices of Biblical times, though this has since been proved to have been a different plant entirely. Aloes are still grown for medicinal purposes. Many members of this large botanical family are cultivated all over the world for their interesting habit and beautiful flowers.

Root of hemlock digg'd i' the dark,
. . . and slips of yew
Sliver'd in the moon's eclipse,
Third Witch – *Macbeth*, IV. i. 25

Upon my secure hour thy uncle stole,
With juice of cursed hebenon in a vial,
And in the porches of my ears did pour
The leperous distilment;
Ghost – *Hamlet*, I. v. 61

Or have we eaten on the insane root
That takes the reason prisoner?
Banquo – *Macbeth*, I. iii. 84

1 HEMLOCK
Conium maculatum

Hemlock has had a sinister reputation for thousands of years, and is reputedly the plant that provided the death-draught of Socrates. The Latin word *maculatum* means 'spotted', and any wild British plant that has purple-blotched leaves or stems is considered unfriendly, even if it is not actually poisonous. Hemlock is not particularly common, and likes to grow on river banks or at ditch-sides; it can also be recognised by its distinctively mousy smell.

2 YEW, HEBENON
Taxus baccata

Hebenon, Hebona, Heben and Yew are deemed by the scholars to be different names for the same tree, because in many Northern European countries, particularly Denmark, the word for Yew is *Heben* or something like it (such as the German *Eibe*) and Yew-poisoning causes similar effects to the manner of death of Hamlet's father. Shakespeare uses the actual word 'Yew' several times elsewhere in the plays, but this short word scans more correctly than would the longer word 'Hebona'. 'Hebenon' is used in some editions of the works, and the word 'Heben' by contemporary authors such as Spenser and Marlowe. Yew leaves are poisonous to cattle, but of the scarlet berries only the seed is poisonous; the fleshy red aril is not.

3 INSANE ROOT
(Henbane)
Hyoscyamus niger

This is another Shakespearean name, which may have referred to any of the poisonous plants then known. Of the native British plants, the most likely candidate is Henbane, because Lyte called this plant 'Apuleia-mania', Gerard called it 'Insana', and it was used by skilled herbalists in former times as a (dangerous) sedative for the insane.

Yea, and to tickle our noses with spear-grass
to make them bleed,
Bardolph – *1 Henry IV*, II. iv. 340

My pity hath been balm to heal their wounds,
King Henry – *3 Henry VI*, IV. viii. 41

. . . no salve in the
mail, sir: O, sir, plantain, a plain plantain!
Costard – *Love's Labour's Lost*, III. i. 73

I meant, plain holy-thistle.
Margaret – *Much Ado About Nothing*, III. iv. 80

1 SPEAR-GRASS
(Couch Grass)
Agropyron repens

The term 'grass' was very loosely applied in the sixteenth century, and could have meant any one of several plants in addition to the true grasses. It has never been conclusively agreed as to which plant Shakespeare knew as Spear-grass, but Couch grass, or Twitch, is considered to be the most likely.

2 BALM
(Lemon Balm)
Melissa officinalis

This plant, which is the Lemon Balm of English gardens, came originally from the Mediterranean area. It was once thought to have many medicinal uses, and was even sold as the Elixir of Life. It can be used to perfume baths and is an important bee-plant.

Balsam or Balsamum was a different product, being made of a mixture of precious oils. It was used for the anointing of kings.

3 PLANTAIN
Plantago major

Valued since earliest times as a herb of healing, the Plantain is a wound herb which can be washed and applied to cuts, grazes, bruises, insect stings and bites.

4 HOLY THISTLE
Cnicus benedictus

The Holy Thistle is another herb of the hot Mediterranean shores which was given its name because it was reputed to cure the Plague. The plant is an interesting yellow-flowered annual thistle, grown occasionally in herb-gardens for its historical interest.

What rhubarb, senna, or what purgative drug,
Would scour these English hence?
                Macbeth – *Macbeth*, V. iii. 55

                . . . these fig-leaves
                First Guard – *Antony and Cleopatra*, V. ii. 355

1 RHUBARB
Rheum rhaponticum

Rhubarb was known only as a medicinal drug plant in Shakespeare's time, and was imported mainly from Turkey, though it was grown in China, India and Tibet. It was not generally eaten as a spring fruit until early in the nineteenth century, though Parkinson, Lyte and Gerard all described it in a hesitant way, and Parkinson had even bravely eaten the leaves cooked in a syrup made from the juice of the stems. This practice is not to be recommended because the leaves are poisonous, containing oxalic acid. The edible part of Rhubarb, the stem, is so acid that it can be used to clean old and stained aluminium saucepans, merely by boiling up the fruit in them.

2 SENNA
Cassia acutifolia

The Greeks knew of Senna and were still using it in the thirteenth century. Attempts had been made to grow the plant in England even in Shakespeare's time, because Senna was well known, even then, for its purgative effect; Macbeth is here asking the doctor to purge Scotland of its enemies as he would purge a body of disease. Senna is a low-growing shrub with golden-yellow flowers native to Egypt and the Middle East.

3 FIG
Ficus carica

In the dark days of European history, the word 'Fig' was a derogatory term meaning a valueless thing, or a thing of little meaning. Shakespeare uses it in this sense in several of the plays – Pistol (*The Merry Wives of Windsor*, I. iii) says 'a fico for the phrase!' Iago (*Othello*, I. iii) exclaims 'Virtue! a fig!' and Pistol again (*Henry V*, III. vi) says 'and figo for thy friendship!'

The expression 'to make a fig' indicated a very vulgar gesture, and, in medieval times to give a fig meant in reality to give a poisoned fig, intended to be fatal for the recipient.

> *If reasons were as*
> *plentiful as blackberries, I would give no*
> *man a reason upon compulsion, I.*
>   Falstaff – *1 Henry IV*, II. iv. 264

1 ANGELICA
Angelica archangelica

A stately plant with a stately name, Angelica differs from its multitudinous relatives in having a completely spherical umbel of flowers – most of the other members of this huge plant family have flat, rayed flower heads, rather like a Japanese parasol.

There is still a considerable demand for all parts of the plant; the candied stems are much used in the confectionery trade, the seeds are needed for the preparation of Vermouth, Benedictine and Chartreuse and the dried root has therapeutic properties.

In former days Angelica was considered to bestow good luck in the spring, and it was carried ceremonially in European 'Maying' processions. The plant was believed to cure the plague, and it is thought to have been named after the Archangel Michael, whose day is on 8 May. Angelica would once have been in flower in early May, whereas, because of the alteration to the calendar in 1732, it now blooms at the end of the month or in early June.

2 BLACKBERRY
Rubus fruticosus

The Bramble is mentioned in the Bible (Judges 9: 8–15) in the parable of the trees who wished to choose a king of their own kind to reign over them. The Olive, the Fig and the Vine all refused the honour for various selfish reasons and the humble and ordinary Bramble was elected king. A Blackberry, Bramble or Briar bush needs no description, having been useful to man since his beginnings. When the remains of Neolithic man were discovered, the contents of his stomach were carefully analysed and it was found that Blackberries had formed part of his last meal – thus even the approximate time of year of his death is known.

There are over 300 species of Blackberry in the United Kingdom and it is often very difficult to differentiate between them, because they frequently hybridise. When picking Blackberries in the autumn it is useful to remember that the crushed leaves possess styptic properties, and a simple poultice may be applied to the bleeding scratches that are so unavoidable.

There is a legend which says that blackberries should not be picked after Michaelmas (29 September) because the Devil defiles the fruit by spitting on them – or worse.

2

1

. . . we have
the receipt of fern-seed, we walk invisible.
Gadshill – *1 Henry IV*, II. i. 95

Yet mark'd I where the bolt of Cupid fell:
It fell upon a little western flower,
Before milk-white, now purple with love's wound,
And maidens call it love-in-idleness.
Oberon – *A Midsummer Night's Dream*, II. i. 165

Be as thou wast wont to be;
See as thou wast wont to see;
Dian's bud o'er Cupid's flower
Hath such force and blessed power.
Oberon – *A Mudsummer Night's Dream*, IV. i. 76

Fern
1 MALE FERN
Dryopteris felix-mas

2 POLYPODY
Polypodium vulgare

There are very many old legends about ferns. It was believed that 'Fern-seed' (which cannot exist, because ferns have no flowers) could confer the gift of invisibility to the finder. He or she must seek the seed on St John's Eve (23 June), and if the proper ceremonial is not observed the seed will vanish on the way home. It is possible that the stories referred to the spores that are found on the back of the fern-fronds after midsummer.

3 LOVE-IN-IDLENESS
(Heartsease)
Viola tricolor

The Wild Pansy or Heartsease is still called 'Love-and-Idleness' in Warwickshire, and 'Love-in-Idleness' in the next-door county of Gloucestershire. The old names for this annual flower of the cornfields are not used as much as they were. There are less flowers among the corn now, and so this so-pretty wild Pansy is almost forgotten except by gardeners who cherish the wild flowers as well as their pedigree relatives.

4 DIAN'S BUD
(Wormwood)
Artemisia absinthium

It is generally believed that Wormwood is the plant that Shakespeare called 'Dian's Bud', because the scientific name of Wormwood comes from Artemis, the Greek name for Diana, goddess of the hunt. This silvery-leaved plant was much used in early medicine, though later physicians discarded it for more effective herbs. Its only certain use in the home was to discourage fleas.

The cockle of rebellion, insolence, sedition,
Which we ourselves have plough'd for, sow'd and scatter'd,
Coriolanus – *Coriolanus*, III. i. 70

Antonio: He'ld sow't with nettle-seed.
Sebastian: Or docks, or mallows.
The Tempest, II. i. 144

. . . of hindering knot-grass made;
Lysander – *A Midsummer Night's Dream*, III. ii. 328

1 COCKLE
(Corn Cockle)
Agrostemma githago

The Corn Cockle is an almost forgotten flower of the English cornfields, because it produced black seeds that speckled the corn of former times, considerably reducing its market value. Among farmers it was regarded as a pestilential weed, and determined and almost successful attempts have been made to eradicate the flower – so much so that it is now quite rare in Britain.

2 NETTLE
(Stinging Nettle)
Urtica dioica

Although Nettles are a sign of neglected places, they are interesting plants with many uses. Nettle-juice is an antidote to the plant's own sting, and the nearby Dock-leaves contain the same substance. A gardenful of Nettles indicates a soil rich in nitrogen. Nettles can be made into beer, cooked as a spring vegetable, turned into a safe pesticide, and the flowers can be used as a healthful hair-rinse.

3 DOCK
Rumex obtusifolius

Almost the only time that Docks are attractive to look at is a fleeting moment in late summer when their leaves sometimes turn a brilliant scarlet. Herbalists of former days used the cooked leaves as a warm poultice for boils, carbuncles and abscesses.

4 MALLOW
Malva sylvestris

This wild flower of hedges and gateways seems to like roadside dust, but will grow large and lush in good garden soil. The flowers were once woven into Mayday garlands, and the whole plant has always been used in herbal medicine.

5 KNOT-GRASS
Polygonum aviculare

Knot-grass is a small and undistinguished plant that grows almost everywhere in the British Isles. Fortunately, even though it might be called a persistent weed, it is still used in herbal medicine to alleviate certain circulatory disorders, and it is useful as an immediate poultice for cuts and scratches.

Here's flowers for you;
Hot lavender, mints, savory, marjoram;
The marigold, that goes to bed wi' the sun,
And with him rises weeping:
Perdita – *The Winter's Tale*, IV. iv. 103

And winking Mary-buds begin
To ope their golden eyes;
Song – *Cymbeline*, II. iii. 25

1 LAVENDER
Lavendula spica

Lavender is often called 'Old English Lavender'; but though it is associated with the street cries of old London the plant is not native to Britain. It was introduced into the country in the sixteenth century from southern France.

2 MINT
Mentha spicata

Mint is so vigorous that it will smother all other plants around it unless it is firmly kept in one place. The easiest way of doing this is to plant the Mint in an old bucket with holes in the bottom, and then to plant the bucket. The Mint will then form a compact and controllable clump.

3 SAVORY
Satureja hortensis

This is a herb-plant that is often grown but seldom used, except in southern Europe where it originated. There are two types of Savory, Winter and Summer, and of the two the Summer Savory (illustrated) has the more delicate flavour.

4 MARJORAM
Origanum vulgare

Sweet Marjoram is another herb-plant of southern Europe, particularly Italy, where the sweetly aromatic dried leaves are known as Oregano. Bee-keepers plant it near hives because the flowers are rich in nectar.

5 MARIGOLD,
MARY-BUD
Calendula officinalis

This old-fashioned cottage garden flower is regaining its former popularity. It flowers continuously from May until October, and will yield a hearty crop of seedlings for the following year. The flower-petals were once used as a harmless food colourant instead of the more expensive saffron. The Marigold has healing powers, and the plant is still used to treat burns and to heal small wounds without a scar. The term 'Mary-buds' is a poetic description of the unfolding flowers.

1

2

5

4

3

Let the sky rain
potatoes; let it thunder to the tune of Green
Sleeves, hail kissing-comfits, and snow eringoes;
Falstaff – *The Merry Wives of Windsor*, V. v. 20

Alas, I had rather be set quick i' the earth,
And bowl'd to death with turnips!
Ann Page – *The Merry Wives of Windsor*, III. iv. 90

Tell him, I'll knock his leek about his pate
Upon Saint Davy's day.
Pistol – *Henry V*, IV. i. 54

1 POTATO
Solanum tuberosum

Potatoes were almost certainly introduced into Ireland in 1584 by Sir Walter Raleigh, and for fifty years after their introduction they were regarded as tropical curiosities from the New World. The Potato is closely related to the Deadly Nightshade, *Atropa belladonna*, and its leaves and berries are almost as poisonous as those of its sinister relative.

2 ERINGO
(Sea Holly)
Eryngium maritimum

The Sea Holly is now an uncommon flower of the sea-coast in most parts of the British Isles, and its metallic blue leaves and flowers are very striking. The plant was much sought after in former days, when the roots were candied for sale as comfits or sweetmeats which had a certain reputation as a restorative of youth.

3 TURNIP
Brassica rapa

It is almost certain that the Romans carried the seed of this worthy if unexciting vegetable with them, and they christened it *Terrae napus* which in time became corrupted into Turnip.

4 LEEK
Allium porrum

The large round heads of Leek-flowers will tower tall among the vegetables of the late summer garden if allowed to do so. They are a handsome sight, and certainly most worthy of the veneration that was accorded them by the ancient Egyptians, and much later on in Anglo-Saxon England. The 'leac-tun' or Leek-garden was the name given to a kitchen-garden, and the 'Leac-ward' was the gardener or Leek-keeper. The Leek is a national plant in Wales, and is worn by the Welsh on St David's Day, 1 March. Pistol is here speaking of the Welsh captain Fluellen.

When I a fat and bean-fed horse beguile,
  Puck – *A Midsummer Night's Dream*, II. i. 45

Evans: *Pauca verba, Sir John; goot worts.*
Falstaff: *Good worts! good cabbage.*
      The Merry Wives of Windsor, I. i. 123

Mustardseed   Dramatis persona, A Midsummer Night's Dream

1 BEAN
Vicia faba

Much myth and legend has grown up around the familiar Broad Bean. For example, the Egyptian priests considered this Bean to be an unclean vegetable, whereas the Greeks and Romans almost worshipped it as a sacred plant.

The powerful scent of a Bean-field in full flower is a great attraction to bees, though, according to an old Leicestershire belief, to fall asleep in a Bean-field was very unlucky indeed. The Bean has always been associated with election by ballot until recent times.

2 CABBAGE
Brassica oleracea

Falstaff is here making a pun on Sir Hugh Evans' pronunciation of 'words'. 'Worts' meant vegetables or herbs.

Today's plant is the cultivated variety of the wild Cabbage, and the Brassica, as it is called by gardeners, has been an overcooked and neglected vegetable for many years. Strangely, it is as a delight to the eye that it is becoming important once more, and there are increasing numbers of ornamental varieties being grown solely for their appearance in the flower-border. These may have leaves of almost any colour, and are often variegated, fringed or frilled.

3 MUSTARD
Sinapis alba

Several types of Mustard are grown today for their seed, and the three most important varieties are: White or Yellow Mustard, *Sinapis alba*; Black Mustard, *Brassica nigra*; and Brown Mustard, *Sinapis juncea*. Mustard has been used since earliest times as condiment and as a medicine, and was recommended by Pythagoras in about 530 B.C. as a good cure for the bite of a scorpion. Mustard has always been an important commercial crop, and in A.D. 301 was listed among food plants being grown in the empire of Diocletian.

In medieval Europe the great Emperor Charlemagne realised the importance of Mustard and ordered it to be grown on his farms and estates. Mustard fields in flower are recognised as an important source of nectar for bees.

The illustration is of the wild Hedge Mustard, *Sisymbrium officinale*.

I knew a wench married in
an afternoon as she went to the garden for
parsley to stuff a rabbit;
Biondello – *The Taming of the Shrew*, IV. iv. 99

And, most dear actors, eat no onions nor garlic,
for we are to utter sweet breath;
Bottom – *A Midsummer Night's Dream*, IV. ii. 42

. . . this gross watery pumpion;
Mrs Ford – *The Merry Wives of Windsor*, III. iii. 42

1 PARSLEY
Petroselinum crispum

Parsley is a strange plant, because for some gardeners the seeds will germinate ahead of the four-week period usually specified on the seed-packet, whereas for others they will not grow at all, even with successive sowings and much care. There is a gardening tradition that Parsley will only grow for the dominant partner of a marriage. Parsley is a valuable source of Vitamin C.

2 ONION
Allium cepa

In the sixteenth century Onions were believed to 'snare the memory and trouble the understanding, but nowadays no casserole or curry would be complete without them. Used medicinally, Onions have an astonishingly remedial effect on a great number of ailments.

3 GARLIC
Allium sativum

Garlic is one of the most powerful and indispensable flavourings available to the good cook, though it is appreciated far more in Southern Europe than it is in the British Isles, owing to culinary misuse and its rather definite and anti-social odour. Many people use powdered Garlic for convenience rather than pressing the fresh cloves, or use too much of it, or cook it in over-heated oil which spoils the flavour. Chewing fresh Parsley is one way of lessening the smell of Garlic on the breath.

4 PUMPION
(Pumpkin)
Cucurbita maxima

Pumpkins are grown more for interest in the British Isles than for culinary purposes, because their bland flavour is so characterless as to need a very definite sweet or savoury addition in order to make a palatable pie.

*Our bodies are gardens; to the
which our wills are gardeners: so that if we will
plant nettles or sow lettuce, set hyssop and weed
up thyme, supply it with one gender of herbs or
distract it with many, either to have it sterile
with idleness or manured with industry, why,
the power and corrigible authority of this lies
in our wills.*
      Iago – *Othello*, I. iii. 323

*. . . when a' was naked, he was, for
all the world, like a forked radish,*
      Falstaff – *2 Henry IV*, III. ii. 333

*Sir Hugh Evans: Remember, William; focative is caret.
Mistress Quickly: And that's a good root.*
      The Merry Wives of Windsor, IV. i. 55

1 NETTLE
Urtica dioica

Nettles were once sensibly used by man as an addition to poultry
and pig food, and eating chopped nettles imparted a healthy gloss to
a horse's coat.

2 LETTUCE
Lactuca sativa

Lettuces contain small amounts of a narcotic juice which can cause
coma, though only if excessive quantities of the 'bolted' plants are
consumed.

3 HYSSOP
Hyssopus officinalis

Hyssop has intense blue flowers which last for about two months in
late summer. It was formerly much used in herbal medicine.

4 THYME
Thymus vulgaris

Thyme prefers the sunniest position in the garden, because it was
originally a Mediterranean plant. It is delightfully aromatic when
trodden on. Garden Thyme is a very important bee-plant.

5 RADISH
Raphanus sativus

There are records of huge radishes weighing as much as 40 lb each.
They were assumed to have powerful magical properties in earlier
times and people were advised to kill vipers by striking them with a
large Radish.

6 CARROT
Daucus carota

Mistress Quickly is here making a pun on both the Latin *caret* and
the word 'root'.

The flowers of the cultivated Carrot are very distinctive in their later
stages, as they form a delicate green cage.

. . . half way down
Hangs one that gathers samphire, dreadful trade!
Edgar – *King Lear*, IV. vi. 14

Let me see;
what am I to buy for our sheep-shearing feast?
Three pound of sugar; five pound of currants; rice –
Clown – *The Winter's Tale*, IV. iii. 38

. . . with a dish of caraways, and so forth:
Shallow – *2 Henry IV*, V. iii. 3

My Lord of Ely!
. . . When I was last in Holborn,
I saw good strawberries in your garden there:
Gloucester – *Richard III*, III. iv. 33

1 SAMPHIRE
Crithmum maritimum

Samphire is a spiky and succulent plant of the sea-coast, and was formerly much gathered for pickling, often from precipitous cliffs. The Samphire-gatherer's trade was therefore a dangerous one.

2 SUGAR
Saccharum officinarum

Sugar had been introduced to Spain long before it was 'discovered' in the New World, whence it was brought to England early in the fifteenth century.

3 RICE
Oryza sativa

Rice was in common use by the sixteenth century, and Gerard had it in his garden, though it did not flower 'by reason of the injurie of our unseasonable yeare 1596'.

4 CARAWAY
Carum carvi

Caraway-seed was very popular in Shakespeare's day, being used in cooked fruit, bread, cakes, and sweets or 'comfits'.

5 STRAWBERRY
Fragaria vesca

The fruit, flowers and leaves of the Wild Strawberry are very pretty and very distinctive, and when used in design they epitomise the country scene.

To whom the heavens in thy nativity
Adjudged an olive branch and laurel crown,
  Clarence – *3 Henry VI*, IV. vi. 33

I was of late as petty to his ends
As is the morn-dew on the myrtle leaf
To his grand sea.
  Euphronius – *Antony and Cleopatra*, III. xii. 8

By heaven, thy love is black as ebony.
  King Ferdinand – *Love's Labour's Lost*, IV. iii. 247

1 OLIVE
Olea europaea

Olive trees had been planted as botanical specimens in England as early as 1640, though there are much earlier 'Leech-books' that required the bark of this tree as part of various herbal remedies. It is therefore probable that the Romans introduced it as they did so many other plants and trees. It is as an emblem of Peace, however, that the Olive is usually remembered, because of the Biblical story of Noah and the flood.

2 LAUREL
Prunus lusitanica

The Laurel of the quotation is the Bay, *Laurus nobilis* (see page 22), but the Laurel beloved by the Victorians for their dark shrubberies is the Portugal Laurel, *Prunus lusitanica*, which has dangling strings of small red-purple berries. There is yet another laurel to confuse matters further, the Cherry-Laurel, *Prunus laurocerasus*, which was introduced into the British Isles some time in the sixteenth century. This has cherry-shaped berries that change from green to scarlet and then to black; these berries are poisonous and contain prussic acid.

3 MYRTLE
Myrtus communis

The Myrtle will flower well in the southern part of the British Isles if it is planted in a sheltered south-facing position or near the sea. The aromatic cream flowers appear late in the year, and were once much used in wedding garlands, wreaths and bouquets.

4 EBONY
Diospyros ebenum

Ebony is a hard and heavy wood of extreme darkness, used by woodcarvers since earliest times for beautiful inlay-work. There are several types and colours of *Diospyros* species, but the black Ebony has always been the rarest and most valuable, and is now found mainly in tropical Africa.

1

2

3

4

Ceres, most bounteous lady, thy rich leas
Of wheat, rye, barley, vetches, oats, and pease;
Iris – *The Tempest*, IV. i. 60

Pimpernel   *Dramatis persona, The Taming of the Shrew*

1 WHEAT
Triticum aestivum

The first cultivation of wheat was an indication of the end of nomadic life and the beginning of a settled existence; for wheat is as old as civilisation itself.

2 RYE
Secale cereale

Rye resists cold well and is often planted in autumn to overwinter; it is the earliest of the cereal crops to be harvested and it does not require the more fertile soil needed by wheat.

3 TWO-ROWED
BARLEY
Hordeum distichon

Barley is grown all over the world, from the northern cold of Norway to the burning heat of India. Barley-bread was common fare in the sixteenth century.

4 VETCH
(Tufted Vetch)
Vicia cracca

Vetches were still grown as fodder crops in the fifteenth and sixteenth century, according to Wilmcote farm records of 1490–91. Wilmcote was the birthplace of Mary Arden who was to marry John Shakespeare, the poet's father.

5 OATS
Avena sativa

Oats have changed in appearance, height and yield very much since Shakespeare the countryman knew them, but a field of ripe oats, all a-tremble, is just as beautiful a sight now as it was in his day.

6 PEASE
(Pea)
Pisum sativum

Peas were not mentioned in old plant-lists before the sixteenth century, but in Queen Elizabeth's reign they were imported from Holland as a dainty dish for the quality. Later on they were grown throughout the country by rich and poor alike.

7 PIMPERNEL
(Scarlet Pimpernel)
Anagallis arvensis

The Scarlet Pimpernel is called 'The Poor Man's Weather-glass' because the flower closes up at the onset of bad weather, or does not even open at all on dull days.

It was the nightingale, and not the lark,
That pierced the fearful hollow of thine ear;
Nightly she sings on yond pomegranate-tree:
Juliet – *Romeo and Juliet*, III. v. 2

. . . where yond pine does stand,
I shall discover all:
Antony – *Antony and Cleopatra*, IV. xii. 1

And Thisby, tarrying in mulberry shade,
Prologue – *A Midsummer-Night's Dream*, V. i. 149

1 POMEGRANATE
Punica granatum

The pomegranate is reputed to have been the 'apple' that Eve plucked from the Tree of Life to give to Adam, and there are many legends surrounding it.

The pomegranate has an important place in Greek mythology, and was blamed as being the cause of winter: Proserpine, daughter of Ceres the mighty Earth-goddess, ate six pomegranate seeds in Hades before she was allowed by Pluto to return to earth and her mother. During the time that she spends with Ceres the world is green, smiling and warm; but for the six months that she has to spend with Pluto in the underworld (corresponding to the six pomegranate seeds) the earth is cold and barren because Ceres is lonely and sad without her.

2 PINE
Pinus sylvestris

The sombre and beautiful Scots Pine is a native British tree, though the original species has almost died out and the limited number of trees remaining are found only in Scotland. The tree was re-discovered and was much planted in the eighteenth and nineteenth centuries as an ornamental. It then developed a different shape to the true species, becoming more flattened at the top. The Scottish trees are slightly dome-shaped.

3 MULBERRY
Morus nigra

Mulberries are the most delicious of soft fruit, and were it not that the trees take so long to grow to maturity they would be more extensively planted today. However, once the tree begins to bear, it will continue doing so for many hundreds of years, growing even larger and more imposing, with its huge and often crooked trunk and handsome foliage. In extreme old age the trees need skilled propping to safeguard them from severe gales. Shakespeare planted a Mulberry tree in his garden at New Place which survived until long after his death.

Let me twine
Mine arms about that body, where against
My grained ash an hundred times hath broke,
And scarr'd the moon with splinters:
Aufidius – *Coriolanus*, IV. v. 112

ASH
Fraxinus excelsior

The Ash is a tree native to England and as such it is surprising that Shakespeare mentioned it only once, in the above passage. Aufidius and Coriolanus, who have been bitter enemies, are now reconciled. In this quotation Aufidius is using the hyperbole of a splintering Ash cudgel to emphasise his former aggression. The Ash is a countryman's tree, strong, close-grained, and normally free from splinters. Because of its resilience and strength it was much used in former days to make most of the tool and implement handles on the farm. Today it is still appreciated for the same characteristics, and is made into the myriad wooden essentials of the leisure industry – cricket stumps, hockey sticks, baseball bats, billiard cues, and oars. Until recent developments in technology superseded it, it was also the wood that was most used to make skis and tennis racquets.

Ash burns well while it is still green, though it is a sin to burn this useful and valuable wood. It is a magic tree, and it brings much good luck. Many Norse beliefs centre round the Ash-tree, *Yggdrasil*, which was regarded in Scandinavia as the beginning of creation. An even-leaved Ash (the pinnate leaves are nearly always uneven in number) brought good fortune to the finder, and Ash 'keys' were carried as a talisman against witchcraft. However, Ash trees seem to be struck by lightning almost as much as Oaks, so it is unwise to shelter beneath them during a thunderstorm. There is an old rhyme to this effect:

Avoid an Ash,
It courts the Flash.

Another weather rhyme is as follows:

If the Oak comes out before the Ash
We shall have a thorough splash;
If the Ash comes out before the Oak
We shall have a thorough soak.

I must have saffron to colour the warden
pies; mace; dates, none, that's out of my note;
nutmegs, seven; a race or two of ginger, but
that I may beg;
　　　Clown – *The Winter's Tale*, IV. iii. 48

Here's the challenge; read it: I
warrant there's vinegar and pepper in't.
　　　Sir Andrew Aguecheek – *Twelfth Night*, III. iv. 159

1 SAFFRON
Crocus sativus

In former days when the summers were much warmer the Saffron Crocus was grown commercially in England at Saffron Walden in Essex, and it had been earlier recorded in English tenth-century Leech books.

The Saffron is a beautiful autumn-flowering Crocus whose distinctive dangling orange-red stigmas have to be hand-picked; it takes about 4,320 of these to make one ounce of Saffron powder, and Saffron was, therefore, a very valuable commodity.

2 WARDEN
(Pear)
Pyrus communis

In Victorian times there were as many as 600 known kinds of Pear, all of them probably descended from the wild variety. Pears are very slow-growing trees, hence the old country saying: 'He who plants Pears plants for his heirs.' The Cistercian Abbey at Wardon (Bedfordshire), which dated from the twelfth century, had three pears as its armorial bearings; these pears were known as Wardons or Wardens, and were still being grown some 350 years later.

MACE, NUTMEG
(3, nut, and 3a, flower)
Myristica fragrans

Mace and Nutmegs grow on the same tree, being different parts of the same fruit, with different perfumes. The outer orange-yellow covering splits open when ripe to show the beautiful scarlet aril, which, when dried, forms the 'mace'; and this in turn encloses the iron-hard 'seed' which is the nutmeg. Nutmeg trees were formerly grown only in the East Indian Spice Islands.

4 GINGER
Zingiber officinale

Ginger was a spice well known to the Greeks and Romans, who took it with them on their travels, and had become a common and very popular spice by the sixteenth century. Gerard attempted to grow it in his garden where it sprouted and produced leaves in its first summer, though winter would certainly have killed this sun-loving plant.

5 PEPPER
Piper nigrum

Pepper was known to civilisation over 3,000 years ago, and was an early import into England. In the middle ages Pepper was used as an item of commerce, and rents and dowries were paid in the then scarce and consequently valuable Peppercorns.

Berowne :   *A lemon.*
Longaville :   *Stuck with cloves.*
                    Love's Labour's Lost, V. ii. 653

1 LEMON
Citrus limonum

A full-sized tree can easily be grown from a lemon-pip sown in a pot. Later on the growing shrub will need to be re-planted in a larger pot or tub, which should be stood out in the sunniest part of the garden in summer, to be returned to a heated glasshouse for the cold winter months. When the sweet-scented flowers form, they should be hand-pollinated to ensure the formation of the fruit. Shakespeare would have known of imported Lemons, and may have seen actual Lemon-trees growing in tubs, often placed alternately with Oranges. Wealthy Elizabethans who collected the vegetable curiosities which were being brought from abroad would have grown both trees, because of their charming characteristic of flowering and fruiting simultaneously. Of all fruits the Lemon is probably the most valuable for the preservation of health. The quotation refers to the Elizabethan practice of making simple pomanders out of Lemons and Oranges into which were pushed dozens of Cloves.

2 CLOVE
Eugenia aromatica

Cloves came from the Moluccas, or Spice Islands, where they have been grown for commerce since earliest times; trading records show that Cloves were being imported into Alexandria in A.D. 176. The Clove that we know is the unopened flower-bud, which has to be picked with great care at exactly the right time.

The history of the Spice Islands clove trade is a disgraceful one. The Portuguese nation controlled the valuable trade in Cloves until 1605, when they were expelled from the islands by the Dutch, personified by the Dutch East India Company whose trading methods were so harsh and cruel that they caused great misery to the native population. To increase the value of the remaining trees, the Company decreed that all other Clove trees, other than those growing on the island of Amboina, should be cut down and destroyed, which not only caused great poverty but struck a great blow to the tribal beliefs of the islanders. In 1770 the French began to smuggle seedling trees out of the islands, and these were planted in Zanzibar; the young trees came to maturity and blossom, and thus the Dutch monopoly was broken. Cloves are used so universally in medicine and all national cookery, that without their powerful scent and flavour curries, baked hams, apple pies, toothpaste, pickles and certain kinds of cigarette would never taste the same.

Rosalind: *I' faith, his hair is of a good colour.*
Celia: *An excellent colour: your chesnut was ever*
the only colour.
As You Like It, III. iv. 11

SWEET
CHESTNUT
Castanea sativa

Shakespeare's Chestnut was the Sweet Chestnut of the illustration.
The other Chestnut that graces parks, avenues and city squares with
its tiers of flower-candles in May is the Horse-Chestnut, *Aesculus
hippocastanum*; this tree was introduced to England at a much later
date, and is thought to have originated in the Balkans.

The Sweet Chestnut was known in England from earliest times,
though it is not native. It is thought to have been brought by the
Romans, who in turn would have known of it first in Asia Minor.
The tree flowers in July, with green-yellow catkins that hang in long
tassels which make a pleasing contrast to the handsome serrated
leaves. The fruit (or nut) is well protected by the green spines of its
'husk' and is ready for eating by the time that the autumn gales have
shaken it loose from the tree. If the Chestnuts have to be knocked
off with long poles they are not ripe, and there is then the
probability of damage to the branches.

The French make a world-famous dessert from the pulp of
Chestnuts, called *marrons glâcés*; the English recognise the usefulness
of the wood and make durable Chestnut paling from it.

Your date is better
in your pie and your porridge . . .
Parolles – *All's Well That Ends Well*, I. i. 172

DATE PALM
Phoenix dactylifera

Dates have been imported into Britain since Anglo-Saxon times, and the indefatigable Gerard made many attempts to grow this graceful tree in his garden. He succeeded in getting his palms to a height of 'three foot, but the first frost hath nipped them in such sort that they perished'. Date Palms of many kinds flourish in the arid and rainless regions of Western Asia and North Africa. The species that is grown commercially for its honey-sweet fruit is the true Date Palm, *Phoenix dactylifera*, which flowers in March and April and whose fruits ripen in October and November. Date Palms are dioecious, that is they need both male and female trees in order to produce fruit, and where one tree grows alone, even in a suitable environment, it will remain barren. Artificial pollination is carried out in Arab countries, but not in India, where the tree does not always do well owing to the high humidity level of the climate. An adult tree will produce about 120 lb of dates, and often more. The half-ripe dates are picked by the simple expedient of cutting off the whole bunch and hanging it in a suitably dry and shady place to ripen fully, though in the case of the more valuable varieties, the dates are picked singly as they ripen. Date Palms were cultivated by the ancients who gave them many different names which referred to the different seasonal state of the fruit, or the tree, or the country of origin, and there are now thousands of varieties. The commercial Date Palm has always been a very important tree, providing essential food for man and beast (the kernels are ground to yield food for camels, and even the dogs eat dates). Huts were made and roofed with the leaves, and the wood was and is used for building purposes. The highly intoxicating drink called 'arrack' is made from the sap which is fermented and later distilled. Crates, boxes and baskets are made from the split leaf-stalks, and rope is made from the fibre which grows at their base.

The illustration is of the Wild Date Palm, *Phoenix sylvestris*, which is cultivated in Europe as a conservatory tree, though in the South of France it grows in the open where it is sometimes planted as an ornamental in parks, boulevards and gardens. It grows wild in India.

Now would I give a thousand furlongs of sea for
an acre of barren ground, long heath, brown
furze, any thing.
    Gonzalo – *The Tempest*, I. i. 71

There is a man . . .
hangs odes upon hawthorns and elegies on brambles;
    Rosalind – *As You Like It*, III. ii. 377

The oaks bear mast, the briars scarlet hips:
    Timon – *Timon of Athens*, IV. iii. 422

1 HEATH
Erica tetralix

It is not certain whether Shakespeare meant what we now know as Cross-leaved Heath, or if, indeed, he meant a flower at all. The 'long heath' of the quotation may well have been a stretch of desolate moorland.

2 FURZE
(Gorse) *Ulex europaeus*

'Kissing's out of season when the Gorse is out of bloom' – so runs the old saying; and, as Gorse is always in flower somewhere, kissing, fortunately, can never be out of season.

3 HAWTHORN
Crataegus monogyna

The red and gold of the leaves and the subdued crimson of the berries are a brief glow in the sombre late autumn hedgerow.

4 BRAMBLE
Rubus fruticosus

By Shakespeare's time the word 'Bramble' had come to mean only the Blackberry (see page 104).

5 OAK
Quercus robur

Hogs were formerly fattened up in the autumn on all the woodland nuts which had a generic title of 'Mast'. The term has fallen into disuse except in the case of 'Beech-mast'.

6 BRIAR
Rosa canina

In this particular passage the 'Briar' is the fruit of the Wild rose, but the words Briar and Bramble formerly meant, as they still do today, any wild, thorny plant.

O'ercome with moss and baleful mistletoe:
            Tamora – *Titus Andronicus*, II. iii. 95

Heigh-ho! sing, heigh-ho! unto the green holly:
            Amiens – *As You Like It*, II. vii. 180

If aught possess thee from me, it is dross,
Usurping ivy, brier, or idle moss;
            Adriana – *Comedy of Errors*, II. ii. 179

1 MOSS
Thuidium tamariscinum

Mosses have many forms and colours, and all are beautiful when looked at under a lens. This particularly bright green moss grows on damp ground, on trees and on rotting wood.

2 MISTLETOE
Viscum album

Mistletoe is a strange parasitic plant, full of legend and mystery. It has always been associated with the Druids and is therefore seldom used in Church decoration at Christmas. The Mistle-Thrush is named after the plant, from the bird's habit of eating the poisonous berries which pass safely through its system, undigested. Mistletoe is most usually found on old Apple trees in the British Isles, but will grow on almost any deciduous tree-bark, though it is seldom found on the Oak.

3 HOLLY
Ilex aquifolium

There are many stories told about the Holly tree, and on the whole they are benevolent. It is certainly lucky to have a Holly growing near the house. Male and female flowers are borne on separate trees, and Holly trees should always be planted in small groups which include both sexes in order to ensure a regular crop of bright berries for Christmas decorations.

4 IVY
Hedera helix

The Ivy's flowers are among the very last of the year, and on warm days in the late autumn the Ivy-bushes hum with the activity of the feeding insects. The conical black berries are poisonous to children, though not to livestock.

5 BRIAR
Rubus fruticosus and spp

To compensate for the wicked thorns of the mature briar there is the summer harvest of beautiful and delicious fruit. The presence of briars and brambles in field and hedge means that there is a plentiful supply of leaves and flowers to provide both larval food and insect nectar for several increasingly scarce species of British butterfly.

Aconitum 94
Almond 22
Aloe 96
Angelica 104
Apple 32
Apricock 22, 36
Ash 128
Aspen 32

Balm 100
Barley 124
Batchelor's Buttons 78
Bay 22
Bean 114
Bilberry 34
Birch 34
Blackberry 104
Box 46
Bramble 138
Briar 42, 138, 140
Broom 54
Bulrush 56
Burdock 66
Burnet 26
Bur 64

Cabbage 114
Camomile 78
Caraway 120
Caret (Carrot) 118
Carnation 88
Cedar 58
Cherry 36
Chequer'd Flower 26
Chestnut 134
Clove 132
Clover 26
Cockle 108
Coloquintida 96
Columbine 52
Cork 62
Cowslip 26
Crab-apple 24, 32
Crow-flower 28
Crown Imperial 38
Cuckoo-buds 30
Cuckoo-flowers 66
Currant 32
Cypress 88

Daffodil 14
Daisy 28, 30
Damask Rose 74
Damson 50
Darnel 66
Date 136
Dewberry 36
Dian's Bud 106
Dock 64, 108
Dogberry 46

Ebony 122
Eglantine 72
Elder 70
Elm 62

Eringo 112

Fennel 52
Fern 106
Fig 36, 102
Filbert 24
Flag 56
Flax 80
Flower-de-luce 84
Fumiter 66
Furrow-weed 66
Furze 42, 138

Garlic 116
Gillyvor 88
Ginger 130
Gooseberry 44
Goss 42
Grass 40

Harebell 16
Hawthorn 46, 138
Hazel 16
Heath 138
Hebenon 98
Hemlock 66, 98
Hemp 94
Holly 140
Holy Thistle 100
Honey-stalk 40
Honeysuckle 62
Hyssop 118

Insane Root 98
Iris 84
Ivy 62, 140

Kecksies 64
Knot-grass 108

Lady-smock 30
Lark's-heels 80
Laurel 122
Lavender 110
Leek 112
Lemon 132
Lettuce 118
Lily 32, 76, 82
Line 86
Locust 96
Long Purple 28
Love-in-Idleness 106

Mace 130
Mallow 108
Mandragora 92
Marigold 120
Marjoram 110
Mary-buds 110
Medlar 54
Mint 110
Mistletoe 140
Moss 140
Mulberry 126
Musk-rose 72

Mustard 114
Myrtle 122

Narcissus 20
Nettle 28, 66, 108, 118
Nutmeg 130

Oak 138
Oats 124
Olive 122
Onion 116
Orange 44
Osier 24
Oxlip 38, 72

Palm 18
Pansy 50
Parsley 116
Peach 18
Pear 34
Pease 124
Pepper 130
Pignut 24
Pimpernel 124
Pine 126
Pink 78
Piony 48
Plane 58
Plantain 100
Plum 36
Pomegranate 126
Poppy 92
Potato 112
Primrose 14, 16
Pumpion 116

Quince 34

Radish 118
Reed 56
Rhubarb 102
Rice 120
Roses 60, 68, 90
Rosemary 50
Rue 52
Rush 56
Rye 124

Saffron 130
Samphire 120
Savory 110
Sedge 56
Senna 102
Spear-grass 100
Stover 40
Strawberry 120
Sugar 120
Sycamore 92

Thistle 64
Thorn 42
Thyme 72, 118
Turnip 112

Vetch 124

Vine 70
Violet 14, 30, 72

Walnut 44

Warden 130
Wheat 124
Willow 58
Woodbine 62, 72

Wormwood 96

Yew 98

Index of Latin Names

Acer pseudoplatanus 92
Aconitum napellus 94
Agropyron repens 100
Agrostemma githago 108
Allium cepa 116
    porrum 112
    sativum 116
Aloe thomsoniae 96
Anagallis arvensis 124
Angelica archangelica 104
Anthemis nobilis 78
Aquilegia vulgaris 52
Arctium lappa 64
    pubens 66
Arrhenatherum elatius 40
Artemisia absinthium 96, 106
Arum maculatum 28
Avena sativa 124

Bellis perennis 30
Betula pendula 34
Brassica oleracea 114
    rapa 112
Buxus sempervirens 46

Calendula officinalis 110
Campanula rotundifolia 16
Cannabis sativa 94
Cardamine pratensis 30
Carex sylvatica 56
Carum carvi 120
Cassia acutifolia 102
Castanea sativa 134
Cedrus libani 58
Ceratonia siliqua 96
Chrysanthemum leucanthemum
    28
Citrullus colocynthus 96
Citrus aurantium 44
    limonum 132
    sinensis 44
Cnicus benedictus 100
Conium maculatum 66, 98
Conopodium majus 24
Convallaria majalis 32
Corylus avellana 16
    maxima 24
Crataegus monogyna 46, 138
Crithmum maritimum 120
Crocus sativus 130
Cucurbita maxima 116
Cupressus sempervirens 88
Cydonia oblonga 34
Cytisus scoparius 54

Dactylis glomerata 40
Daucus carota 118
Delphinium orientale 80
Dianthus allwoodii 78

caryophyllus 88
Diospyros ebenum 122
Dryopteris felix-mas 106

Endymion non-scriptus 16
Erica tetralix 138
Eryngium maritimum 112
Eugenia aromatica 132

Ficus carica 36, 102
Foeniculum vulgare 52
Fragaria vesca 120
Fraxinus excelsior 128
Fritillaria imperialis 38
    meleagris 26
Fumaria officinalis 66

Hedera helix 62, 140
Heracleum sphondyllium 64
Holcus lanatus 40
Hordeum distichon 124
Hyoscyamus niger 98
Hyssopus officinalis 118

Ilex aquifolium 140
Iris germanica 84
    pseudacorus 56
    xiphioides 84

Juglans regia 44

Lactuca sativa 118
Lamium album 28
Laurus nobilis 18, 122
Lavendula spica 110
Lilium candidum 76
    martagon 82
    pyrenaicum 82
Linum narbonnense 80
Lolium temulentum 66
Lonicera periclymenum 62, 72
Luzula sylvatica 56
Lychnis flos-cuculi 28

Malus domestica 32
    sylvestris 24
Malva sylvestris 108
Mandragora officinarum 92
    vernalis 92
Melissa officinalis 100
Mentha spicata 110
Mespilus germanica 54
Morus nigra 126
Myristica fragrans 130
Myrtus communis 122

Narcissus poeticus 20
    pseudo-narcissus 14

Olea europaea 122
Onopordum acanthium 64
Orchis mascula 28
Origanum vulgare 110
Oryza sativa 120

Paeonia officinalis 48
Papaver somniferum 92
Petroselinum crispum 116
Phoenix dactylifera 136
Phoenix sylvestris 136
Phragmites communis 56
Pinus sylvestris 126
Piper nigrum 130
Pisum sativum 124
Plantago major 100
Platanus x acerifolia 58
Polygonum aviculare 108
Polypodium vulgare 106
Populus tremula 32
Poterium sanguisorba 26
Primula elatior 38, 72
    veris 26
    vulgaris 14, 16
Prunus armeniaca 22, 36
    avium 36
    domestica 36
    dulcis 18
    insititia 50
    lusitanica 122
    persica 18
    spinosa 42
Punica granatum 126
Pyrus communis 34, 130

Quercus robur 138
    suber 62

Ranunculus acris 30
    acris flora plena 78
    repens 66
Raphanus sativus 118
Rheum rhaponticum 102
Ribes rubrum 32
    uva-crispa 44
Rosa x alba maxima 60, 90
    arvensis 72
    canina 138
    centifolia 74
    centifolia muscosa 74
    damascena 74
    damascena versicolor 60
    gallica versicolor 60, 90
    officinalis 60, 90
    rubiginosa 72
    willmottiae 68
Rosmarinus officinalis 50
Rubus spp 42
    caesius 36

fruticosus 104, 138, 140
Rumex conglomeratus 64
  obtusifolius 108
Ruta graveolens 52

Saccharum officinarum 120
Salix alba 58
  caprea 18
  viminalis 24
Sambucus nigra 70
Satureja hortensis 110
Scirpus lacustris 56
Secale cereale 124
Sinapis alba 114
Sisymbrium officinale 114

Solanum tuberosum 112

Taxus baccata 98
Thelycrania sanguinea 46
Thuidium tamariscinum 140
Thymus drucei 72
  vulgaris 118
Tilia x europaea 86
Trifolium pratense 26, 40
  repens 26, 40
Triticum aestivum 124
Tropaeolum majus 80
Typha latifolia 56

Ulex europaeus 42, 138

Ulmus procera 62
Urtica dioica 66, 108, 118

Vaccinium myrtillus 34
Vicia cracca 124
  faba 114
Viola canina 72
  odorata 14, 30
  riviniana 30
  tricolor 106
  wittrockiana 50
Viscum album 140
Vitis vinifera 70

Zingiber officinale 130

Bibliography

Clapham, Tutin, Warburg, *Flora of the British Isles*, Cambridge University Press, 1962

Crane, Walter, *Flowers from Shakespeare's Gardens*, Cassell, 1906

Culpeper, Nicholas, *Culpeper's Complete Herbal*, Thomas Kelly (London), 1828

de Bray, Lys, *The Wild Garden*, Weidenfeld & Nicholson, 1978

Ellacombe, Rev. Henry N., M.A., *The Plant-Lore and Garden Craft of Shakespeare*, printed for
  W. Satchell and Co. and sold by Simkin, Marshall and Co., 1884

Ellacombe, Rev. H.N., *Plant-Lore of Shakespeare*, Edward Arnold, 1896

Grieve, M., F.R.H.S., *A Modern Herbal*, Jonathan Cape, 1974

Grigson, Geoffrey, *The Englishman's Flora*, Paladin, 1975

Grindon, L.H., *Shakspere Flora*, Palmer and Howe, 1883

Hinman, Charlton, *The First Folio of Shakespeare*, W.W. Norton & Co. Inc., 1968

Moldenke, H.N., Ph. D. and Moldenke, Alma L., B.A., *Plants of the Bible*, The Ronald Press
  Co., 1952

Polunin, Oleg and Everard, Barbara, *Trees and Bushes of Europe*, Oxford University Press, 1978

Putnam, Clare, *Flowers and Trees of Tudor England*, Hugh Evelyn Ltd., 1972

Rowse, A.L., *Shakespeare's Sonnets – Problems Solved*, Macmillan 1964

Savage, F.G., *Flora and Folklore of Shakespeare*, E. J. Burrow, 1923

Schoenbaum, S., *William Shakespeare (A Compact Documentary Life)*, Oxford University Press,
  1978

Shakespeare, William, and Fletcher, John, *Two Noble Kinsmen*, Edward Arnold, 1970

Sinclair Rohde, Eleanour, *Shakespeare's Wild Flowers, Fairy Lore, Gardens, Herbs, Gatherers of
  Simples and Bee Lore*, The Medici Society Ltd., 1935

Singleton, Esther, *Shakespeare Garden*, Cecil Palmer, 1932

Spevack, Marvin, *The Harvard Concordance to Shakespeare*, Belknap Press of Harvard University,
  1973

Stuart Thomas, Graham, *The Old Shrub Roses*, J.M. Dent and Sons Ltd., 1979

Synge, Patrick M., *Dictionary of Gardening*, Oxford University Press, 1956

Thiselton Dyer, Rev. T.F., *Folk-Lore of Shakespeare*, Griffith and Farran, 1883

Thomson, William A.R. (Ed.), *Healing Plants – A Modern Herbal*, Macmillan, 1964

Woodward, Marcus, *Gerald's Herball*, Gerald Howe, 1972

The International Book of Wood, Mitchell Beazley, 1979